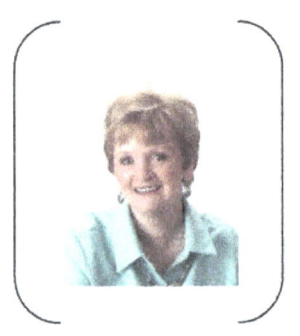

CZT, Jeanne Paglio is an artist, designer and author. She has written and illustrated six tangling books. She is also the author of five mystery novels under the pen name J.M. Griffin.
You can reach Jeanne at Artistry9@aol.com
www.decorativeartistry.us

Tangling is a perfect way to free yourself from the everyday stresses in life. From children through mature adults, the Zentangle method of artful relaxation has helped many to become better at handling their stress, to focus better, renew their spirits and reveal the artist within themselves. So many times I have heard people say "Oh, I can't draw". Now you can by using this art form to help you relax and tangle your way to relief from everyday anxieties and journey to a healthier YOU. Tangling isn't a cure for life's problems, but an aid in helping to take a break from them, even if it is just for a brief period of time. Besides that, tangling is fun and there is NO WRONG WAY to do it!
ꝺꝺꝺ

My thanks go to Maria Thomas and Rick Roberts for sharing their wonderful world of Zentangle. I am hooked on this art form and find I like no other as well. They are an inspiration. I will always be thankful for meeting them and becoming a certified Zentangle teacher.

For more information on Zentangle go to: www.Zentangle.com
You'll find supplies, classes, instructors, tangles and more...

Tangling can be done on just about any surface imaginable. Paper is a great way to start, but by thinking outside the box, so much more is possible. There are mediums that work better for specific surfaces. Take sneakers for example, using a waterproof pen on them would be wise. This makes them washable. The same can be said for clothing or fabric in general. Use a pen that doesn't bleed and will hold up to washing/cleaning and wear.
When using paint as a base color before tangling, make sure it is compatible with the pens. Play around with pens, mediums and surfaces before getting too carried away. This way you'll know what to expect. ♥ On the following pages, I share the mediums and pens I have used. So let's get started, shall we?

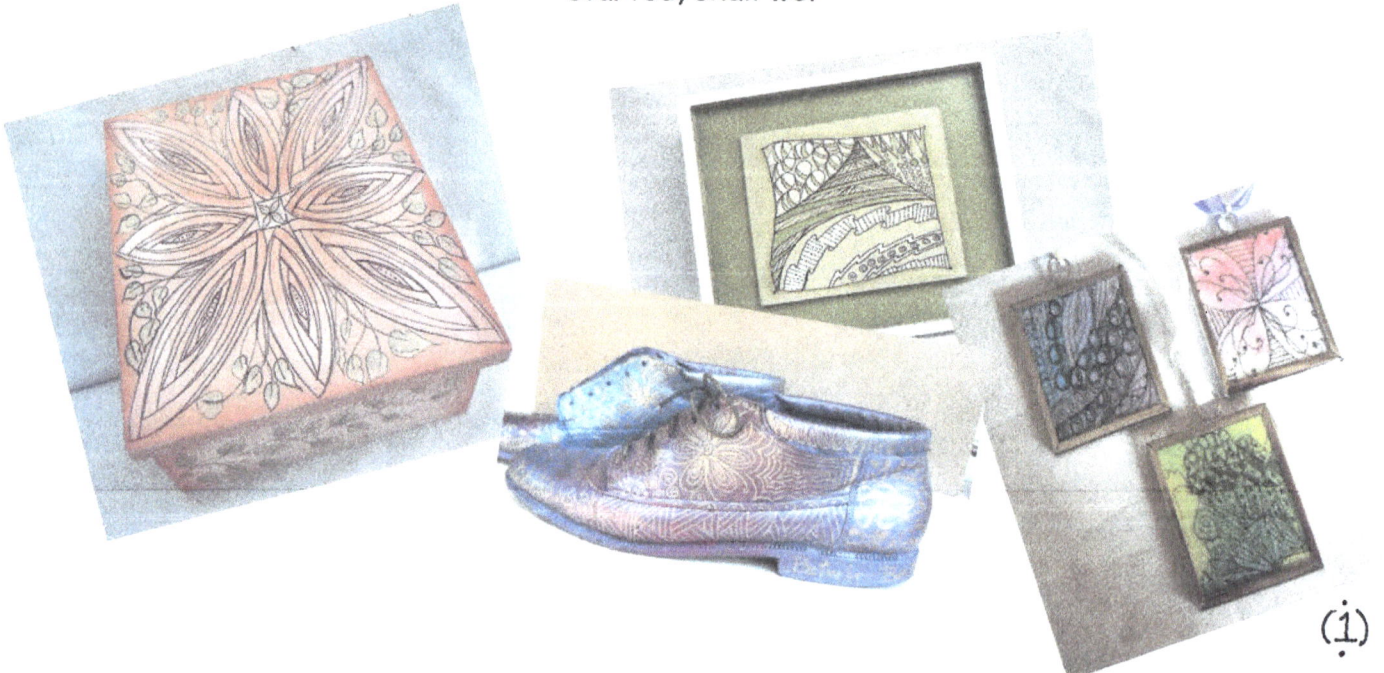

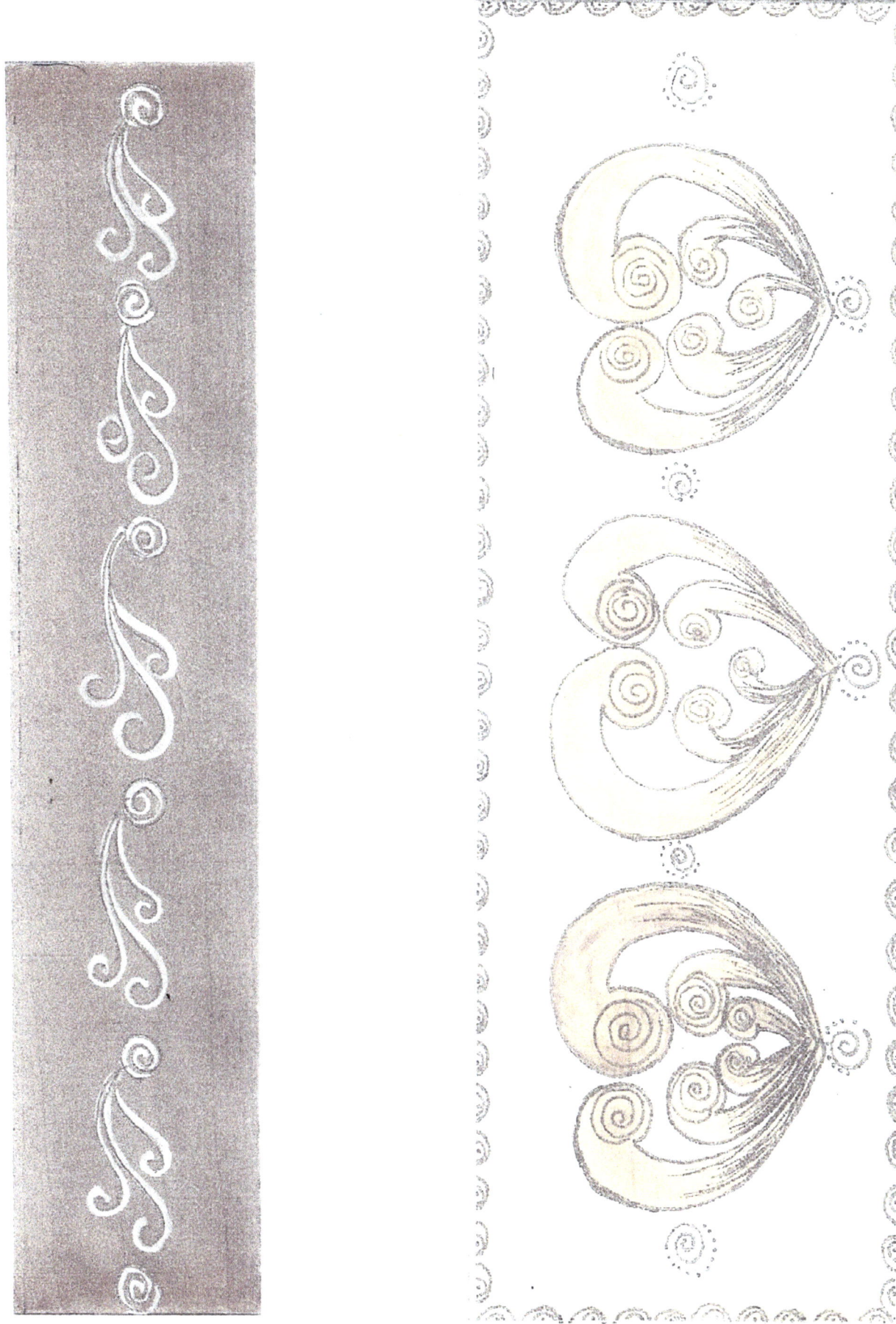

Pencil boxes like these can be used for storing treasures of all types.
This box is available at www.JBWood.com

(2)

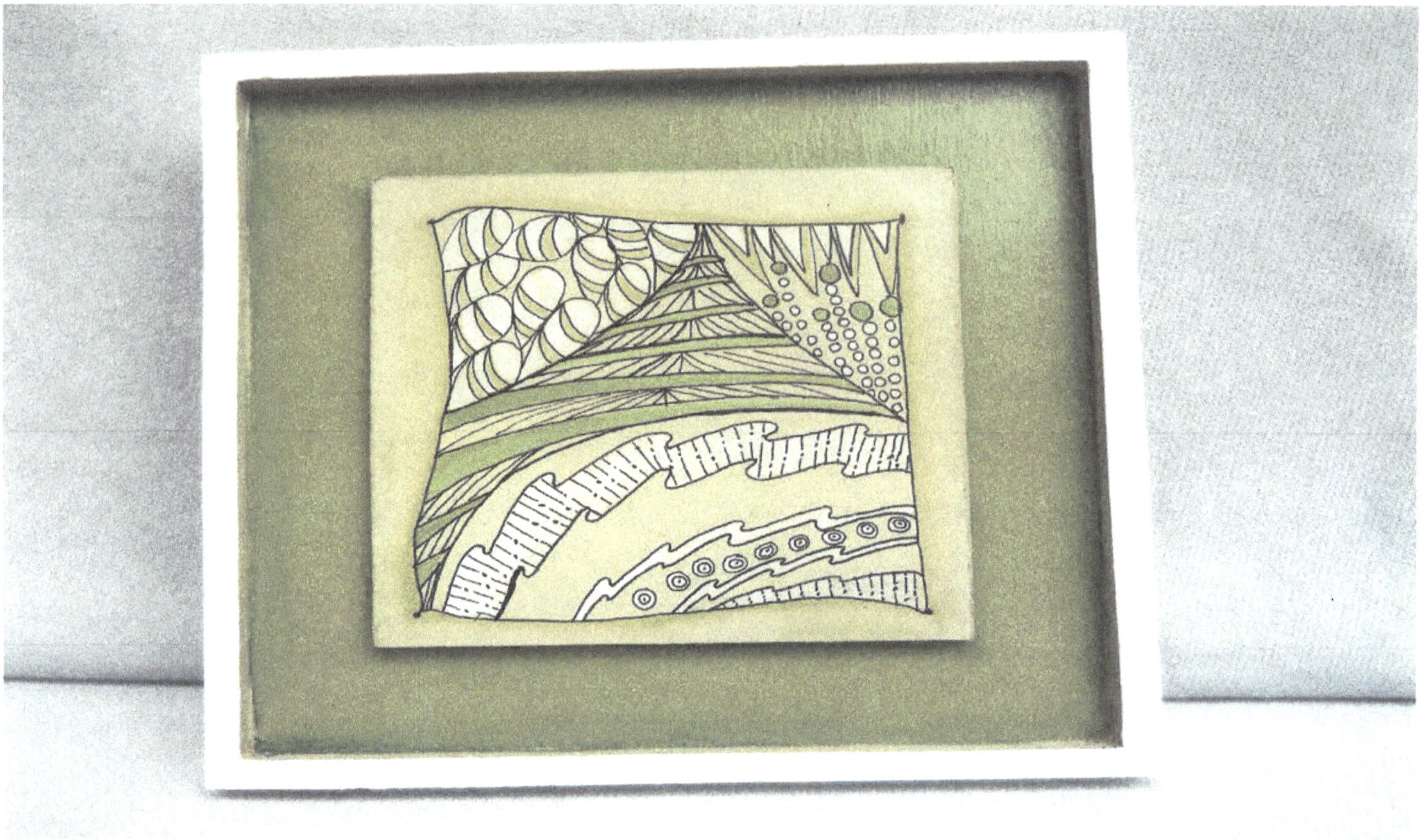

Working on the wooden square was like working on a paper tile. The interior background was painted a light color fist. Once the design was inked, then a wash of colors was added to make it more fun and interesting. Once the square was finished, the frame was painted and the square was then glued into place. A spray varnish finished the it off giving it shine. The design parts are below. Practice them on the next page. Have some fun...breathe...relax...laugh out loud!!

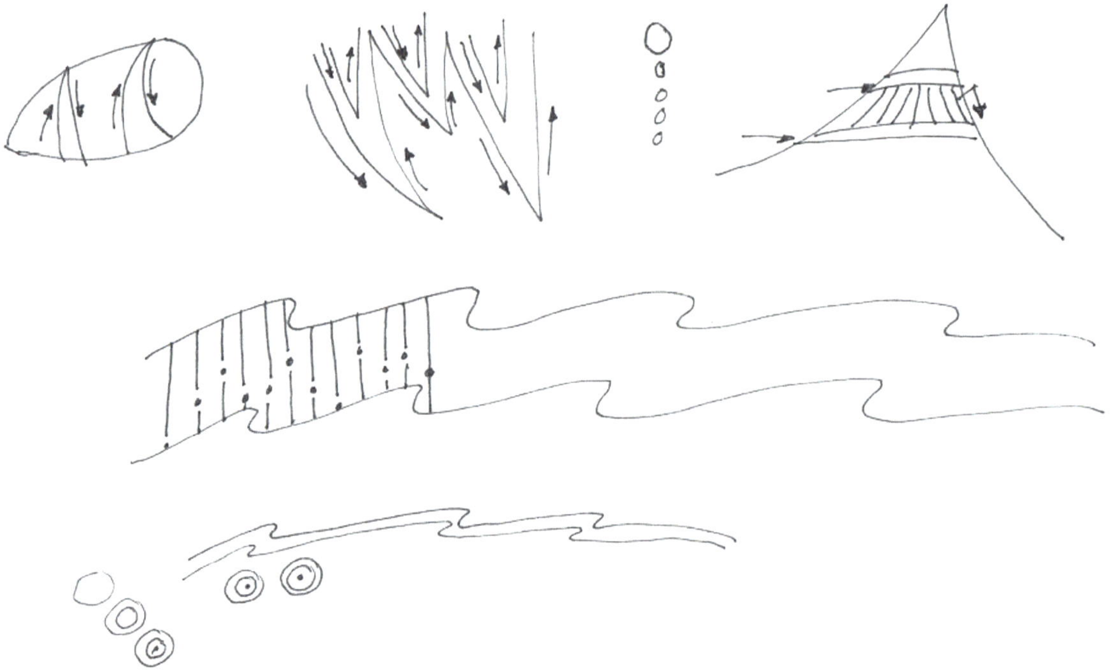

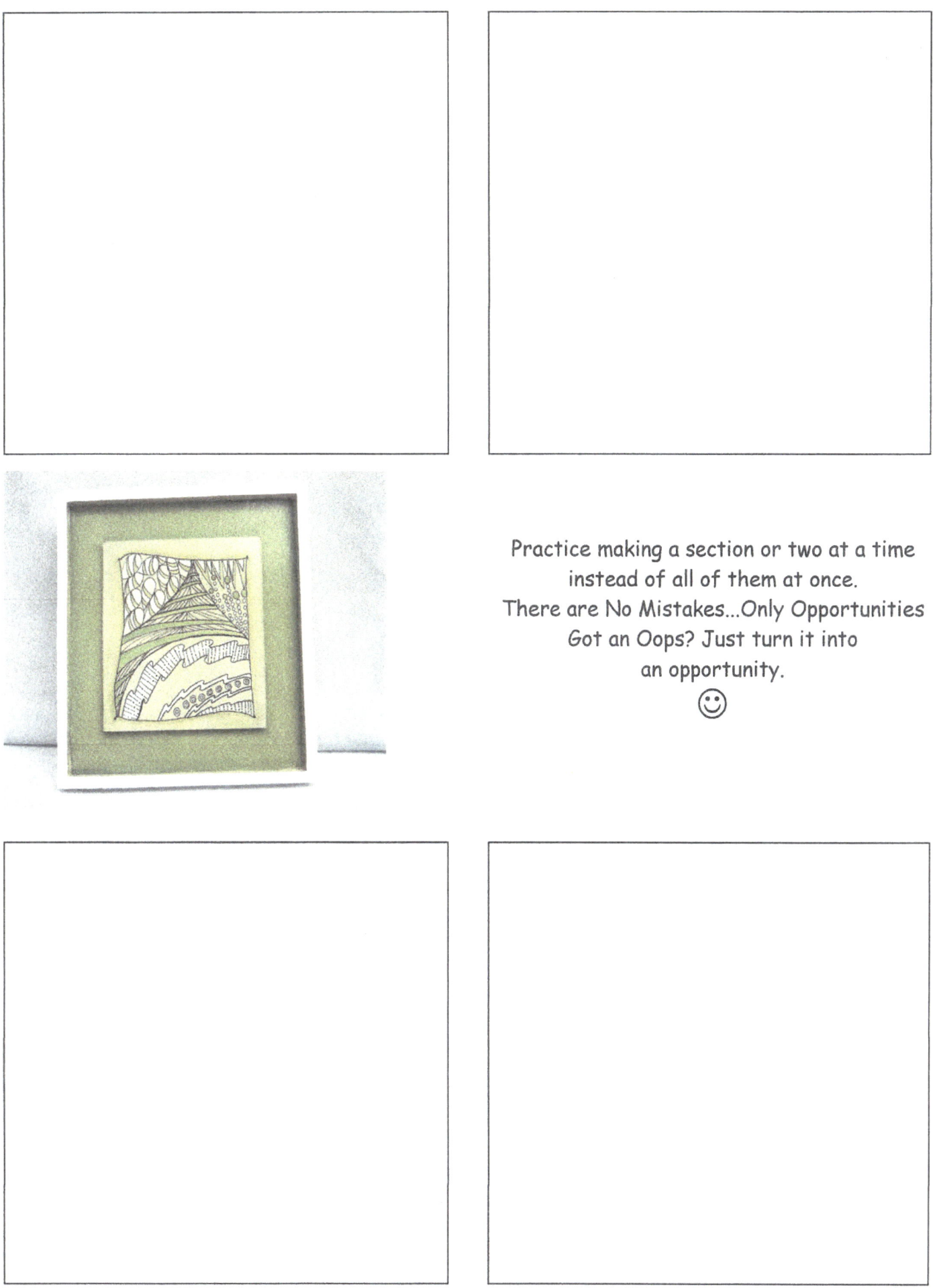

Practice making a section or two at a time
instead of all of them at once.
There are No Mistakes...Only Opportunities
Got an Oops? Just turn it into
an opportunity.
☺

Butterfly, butterfly, my sweet,
lovely butterfly....

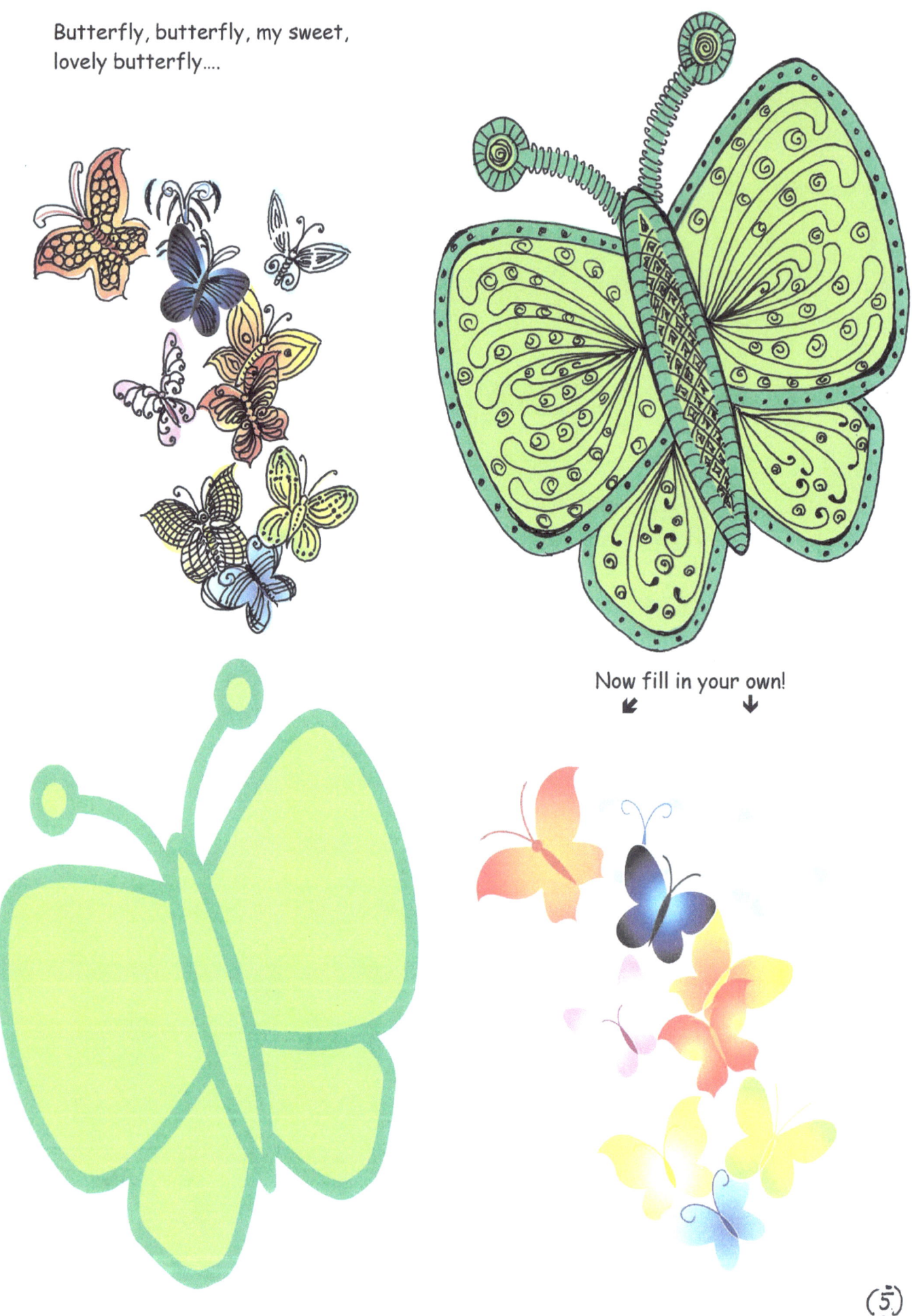

Now fill in your own!

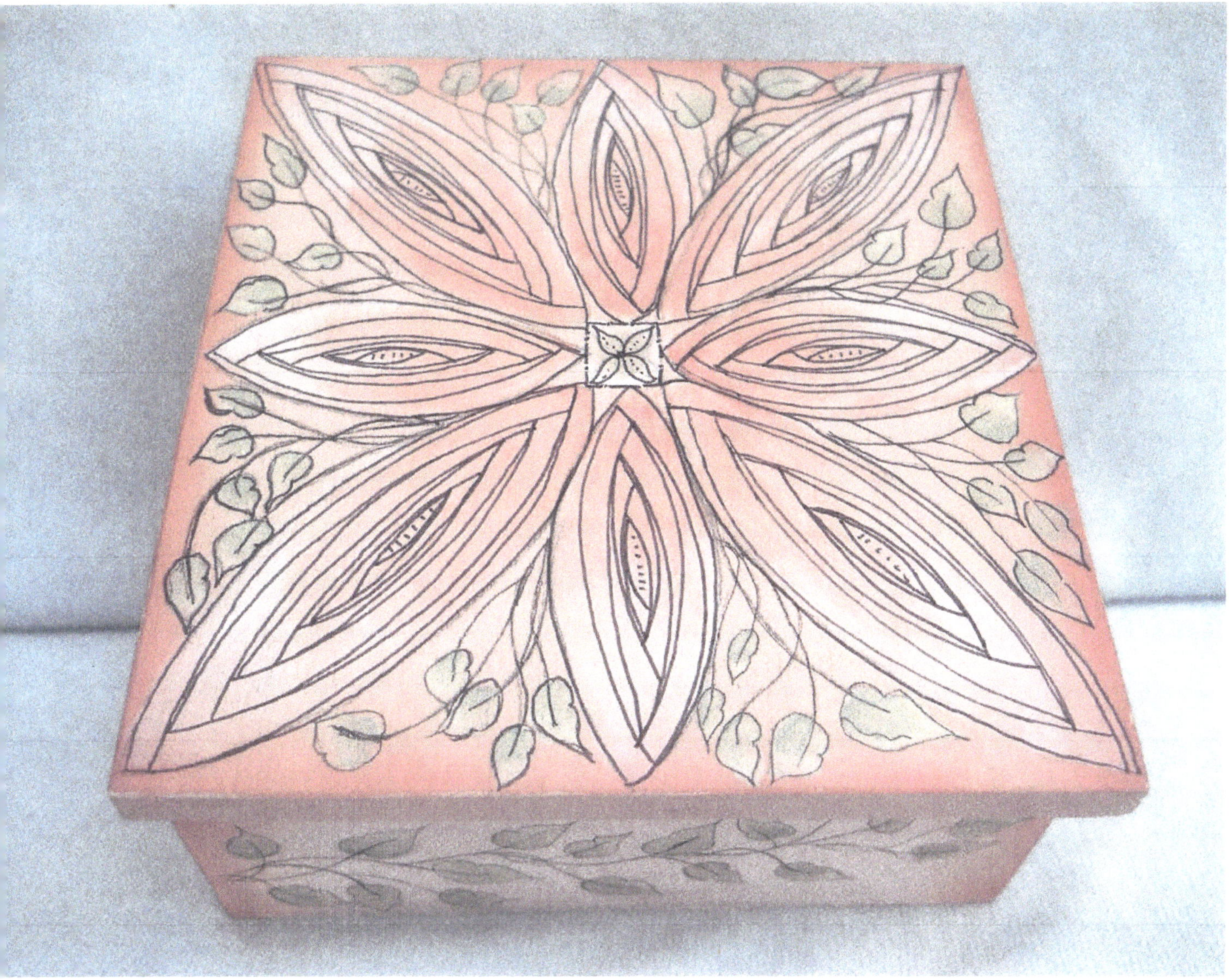

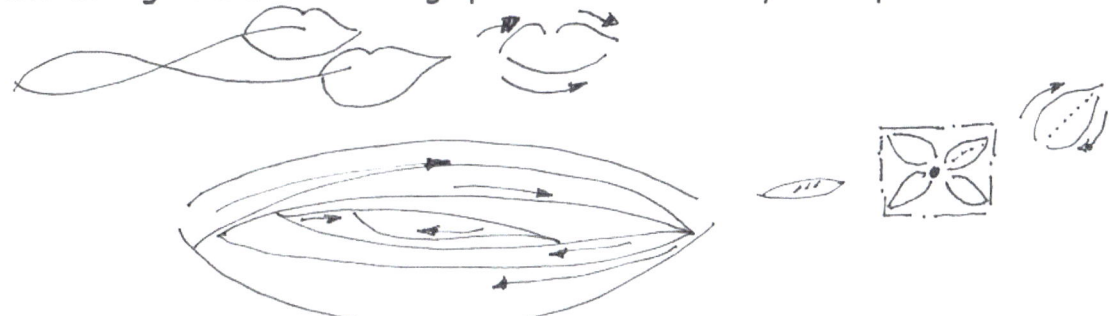

Acrylic paint was used on this box. I painted it with a light color and then rubbed a darker color in the same color family along the edges, softening it as I went. If you have painted before, side load a brush and float the color along the edges of the surface. If you don't paint, but want the same look, then moisten a paper towel slightly with water. Pick up the color and gently rub it onto the surface edges using a circular motion. Do the same thing in the middle of the box lid rubbing outward until the color fades. Dry the surface completely and add the design beginning in the center and moving outward. The design parts are below and you can practice them on the next page.

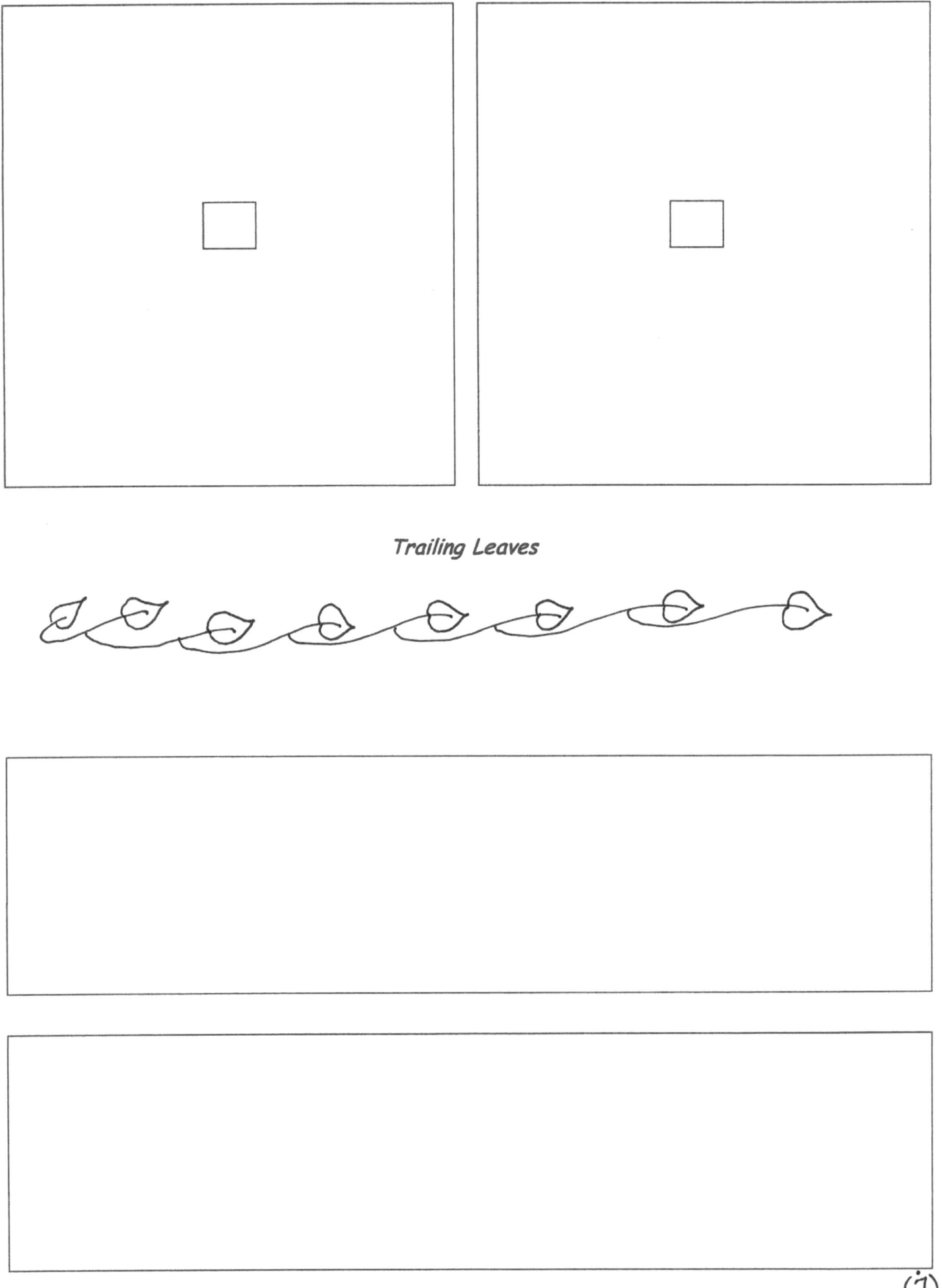

Trailing Leaves

endants, like those below, look complicated, but they aren't. I used 140# watercolor paper, water thinned acrylic paint, and Sakura pens to tangle them. The memory frames are from Inkssentials by Ranger. They have a side clasp to open them. Measure the area inside the frame, cut the watercolor paper and a piece of craft foam for backing. All these items can be found in the craft section of stores. After thinning the paint with water to a milky consistency, spread it over the paper using a paint brush. To vary the colors, overlap them. When the paper dries <u>completely</u>, ink it with a design. After the ink sets, spray the piece with a light mist of matte acrylic varnish. This seals the ink so it won't run when a heavy coat of varnish is added along with a sprinkle of glitter. Once the piece is dry and ready for assembly, gather the craft foam and the painted piece, line them up and put them inside the frame. Close the clasp, add a piece of ribbon as a necklace and it's done!!!

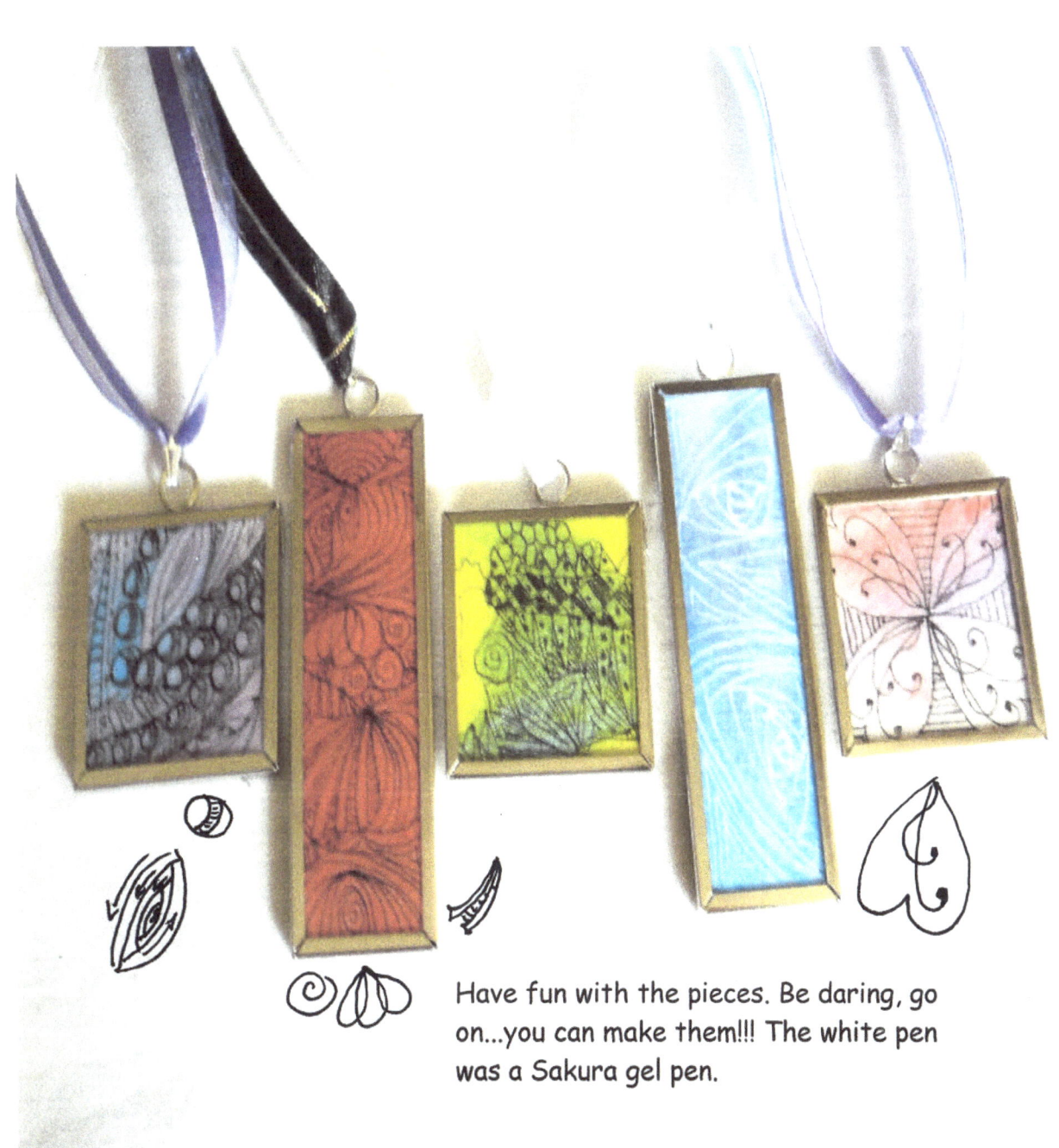

Have fun with the pieces. Be daring, go on...you can make them!!! The white pen was a Sakura gel pen.

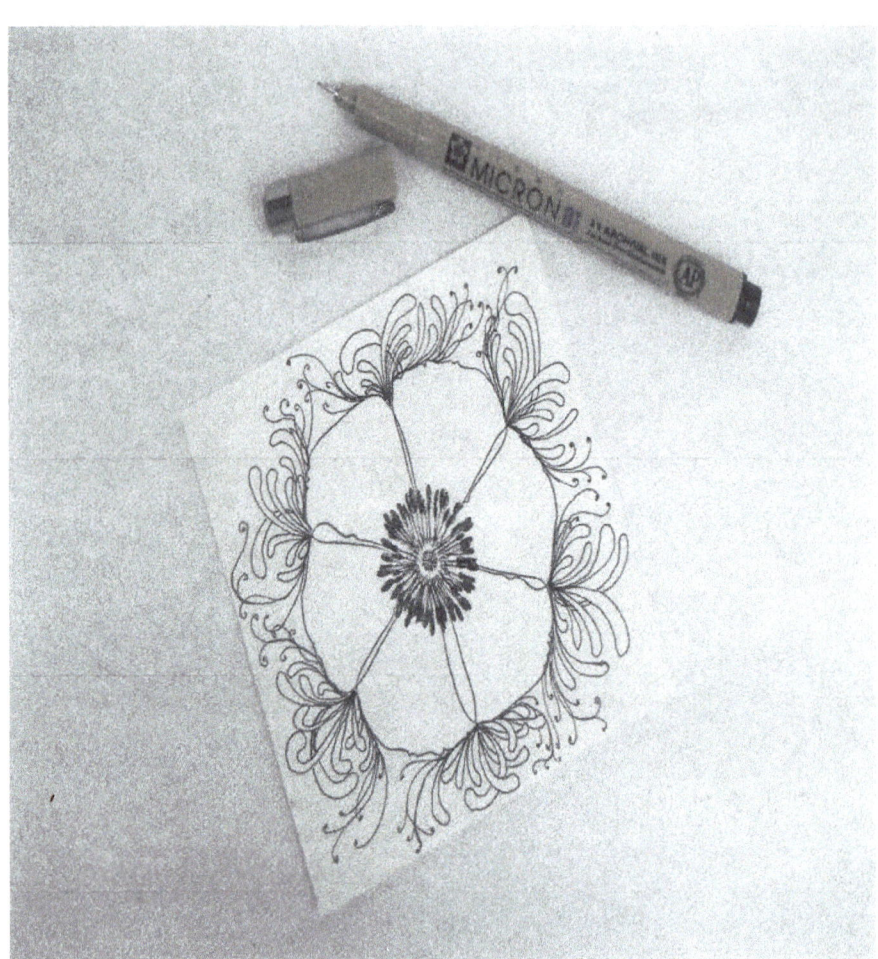

The flower itself was rubber stamped using an archival ink so it wouldn't run when it was painted with watercolors.

The trim around the flower edges were added using a Micron 01 black pen. Below are examples of the trims for your use. ↓

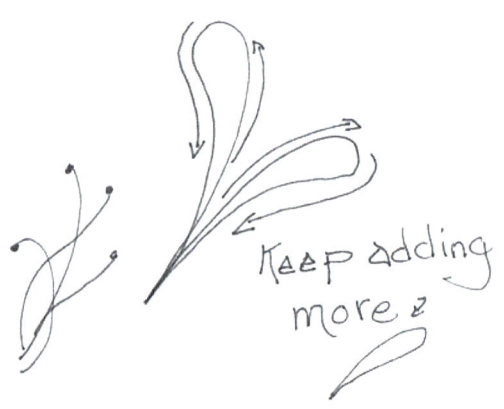

Keep adding more ?

Color was added using watercolor pencils. Then a water brush was used. This brush is great due to the water being in the clear section so you can squeeze a little or a lot of water into the brush. Be careful to hold it gently. Too much water causes the color to *run away*. Here is an example of how the pencil color moves when wet. I used Derwent brand, but other brands work well, too. ↓

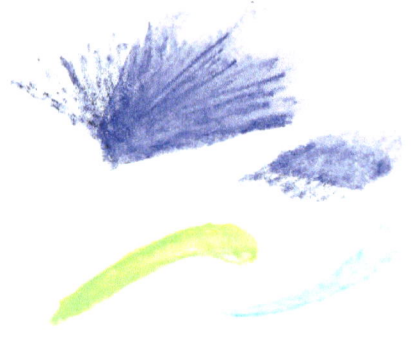

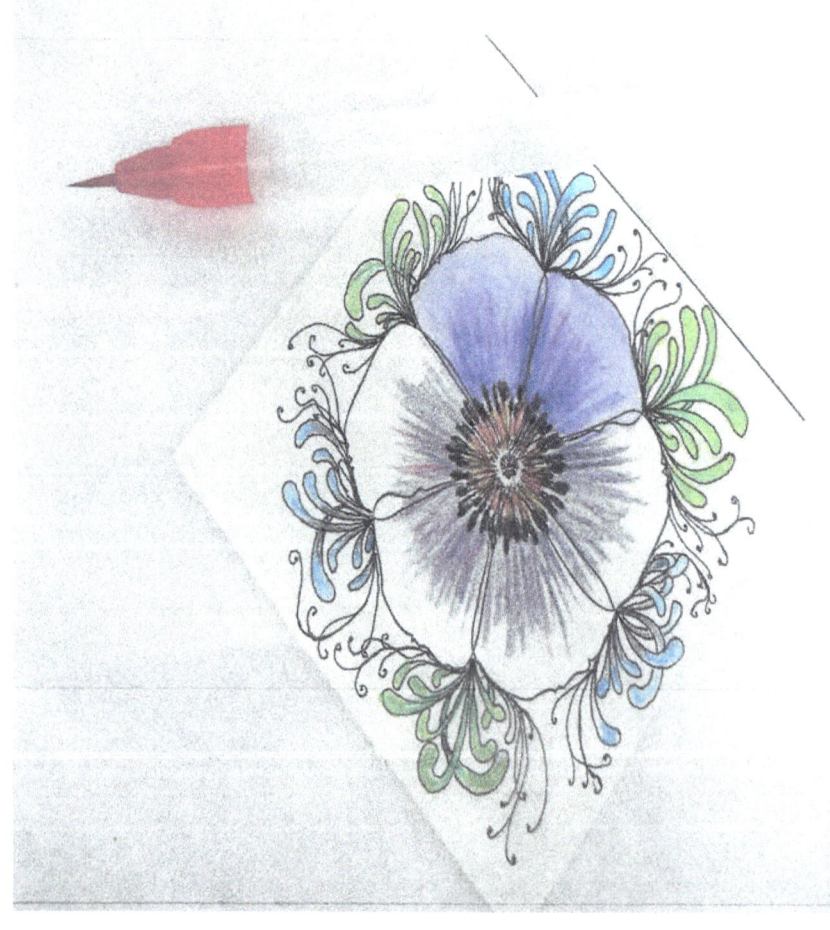

Work with your own style on the stamped flowers below or use the trim designs from the previous page.

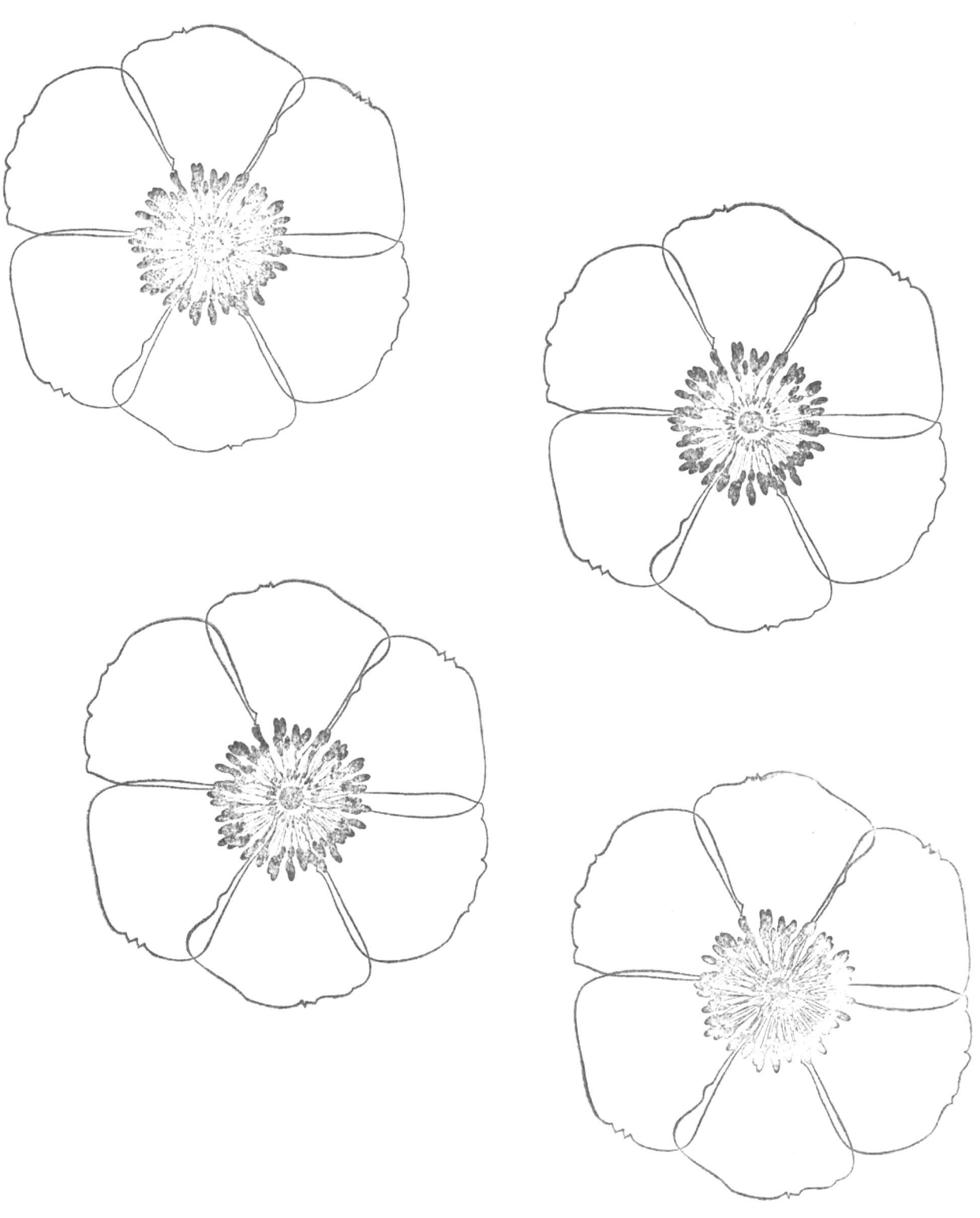

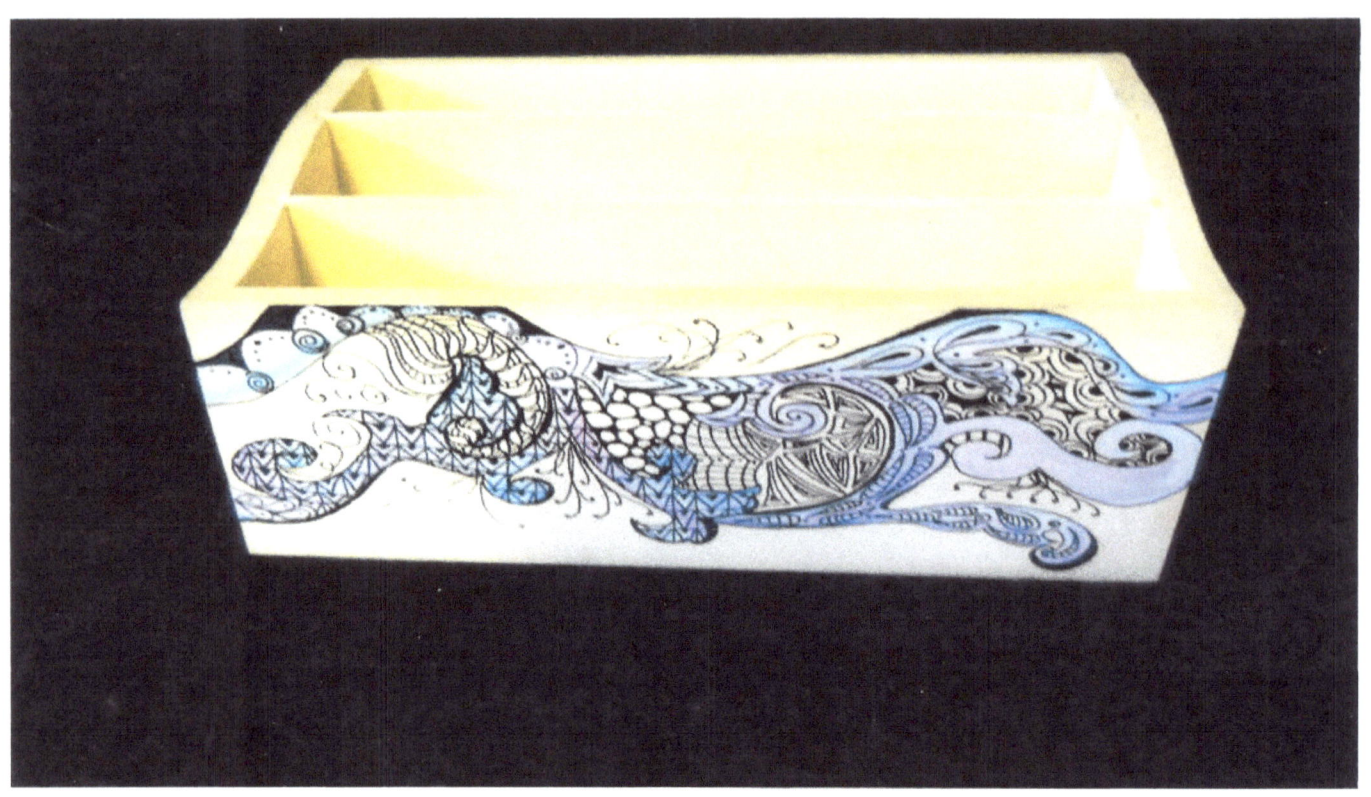

I was asked to participate in a Spring Festival (held by J.B. Wood Products in Attleboro, MA) this spring (www.jbwood.com). Every year the company hosts several artists who offer an hour long class to the people who attend and shop. I came up with this design when they gave me the surface (a TV remove holder) to paint. It isn't a difficult project, the colors are simple and the box is nicely sized. If you have another surface to use this design on, feel free to do so. Paint the box, shade around the edges with a brush or sea sponge using a color a shade or two darker than the base color. Apply the design using wax free transfer paper. Thin the colors of your choice with water and fill in the design using a round brush. Overlap the colors for additional interest. When the paint is dry, ink the design using a Micron 01 pen or a black Sharpie fine-point pen. Spray to finish using matte spray varnish. All done!!!!

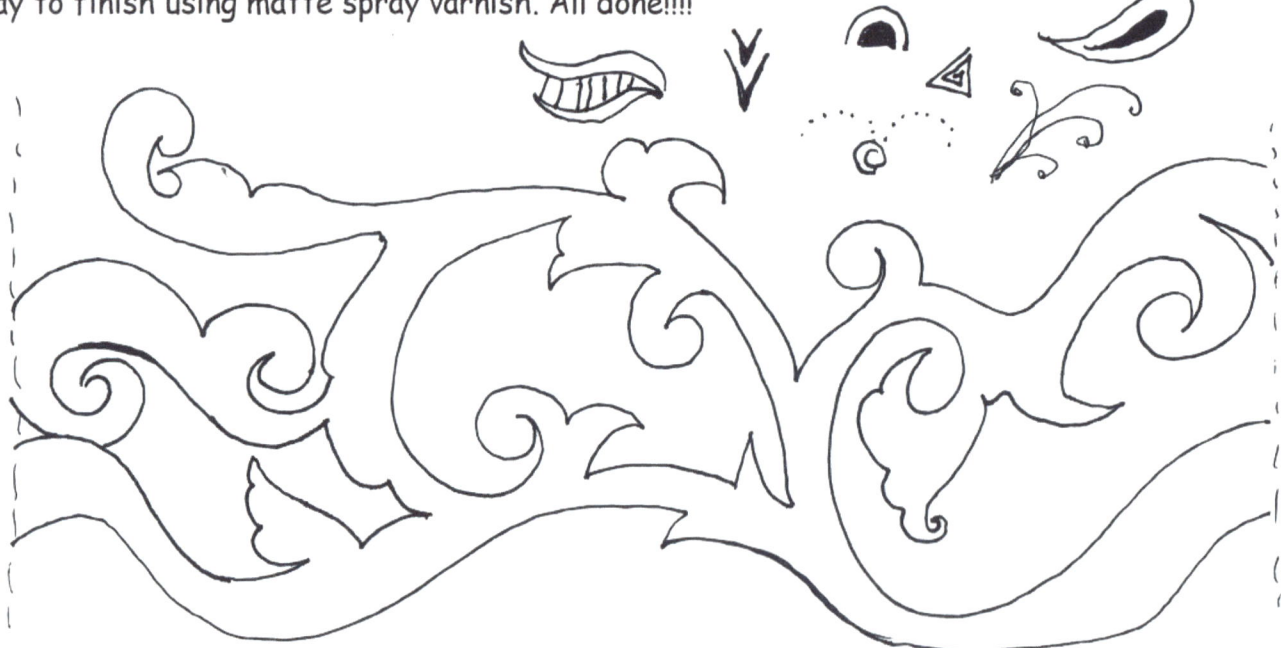

Picture Frames!

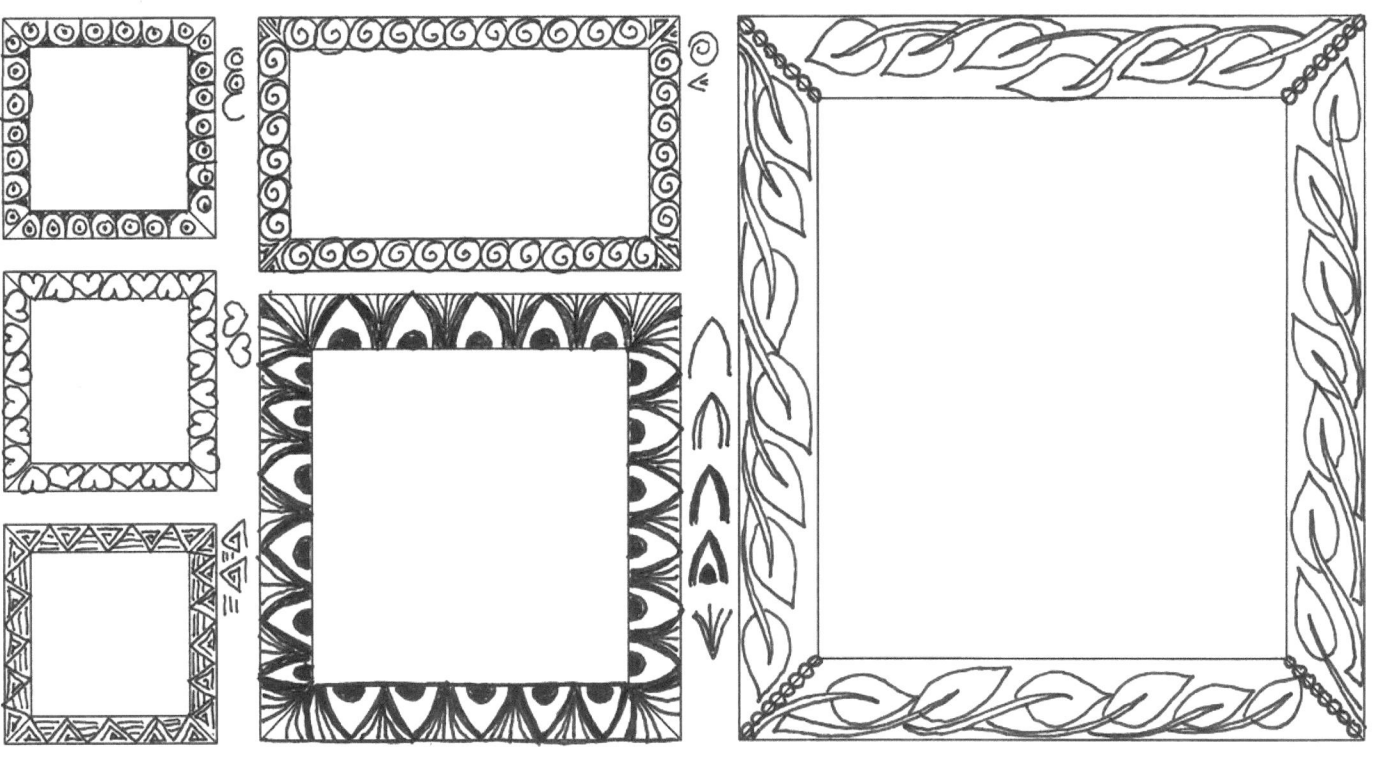

✧ Add your designs to the ones below. ✧

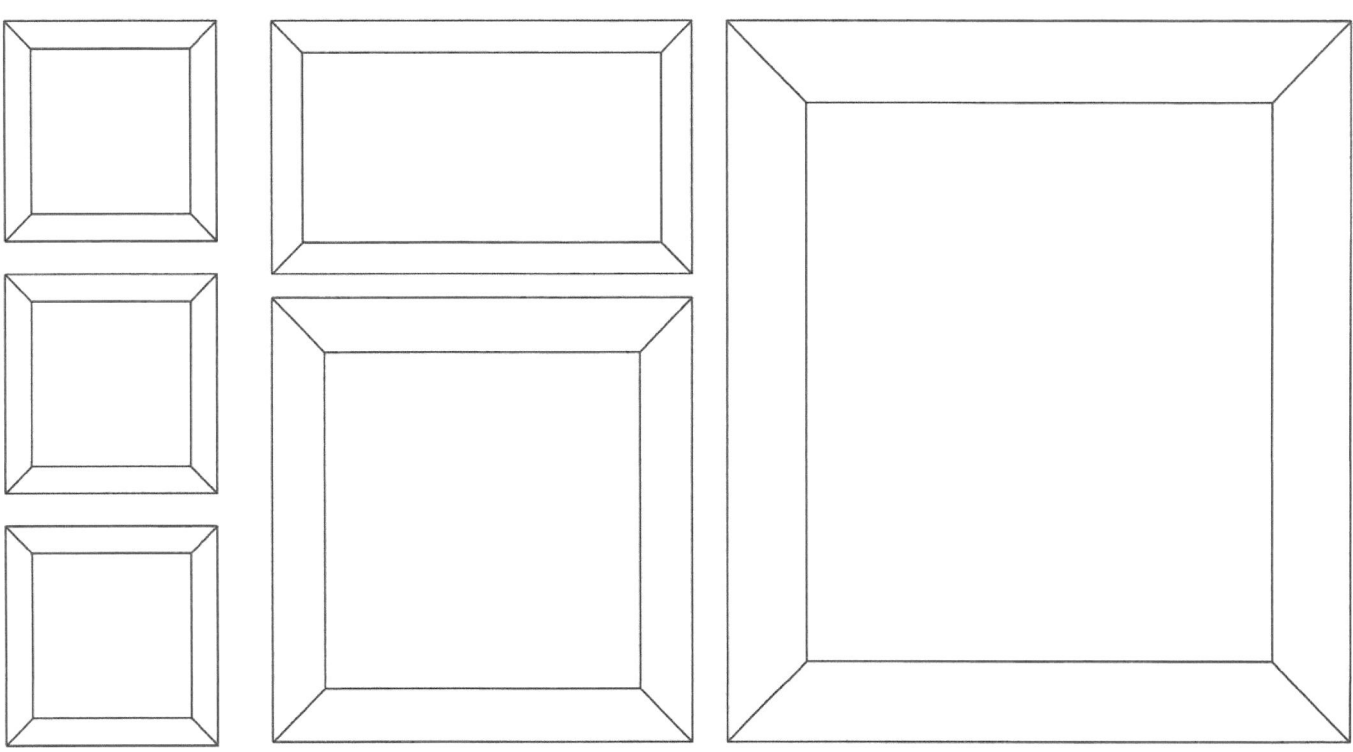

Pictures are windows to the past...

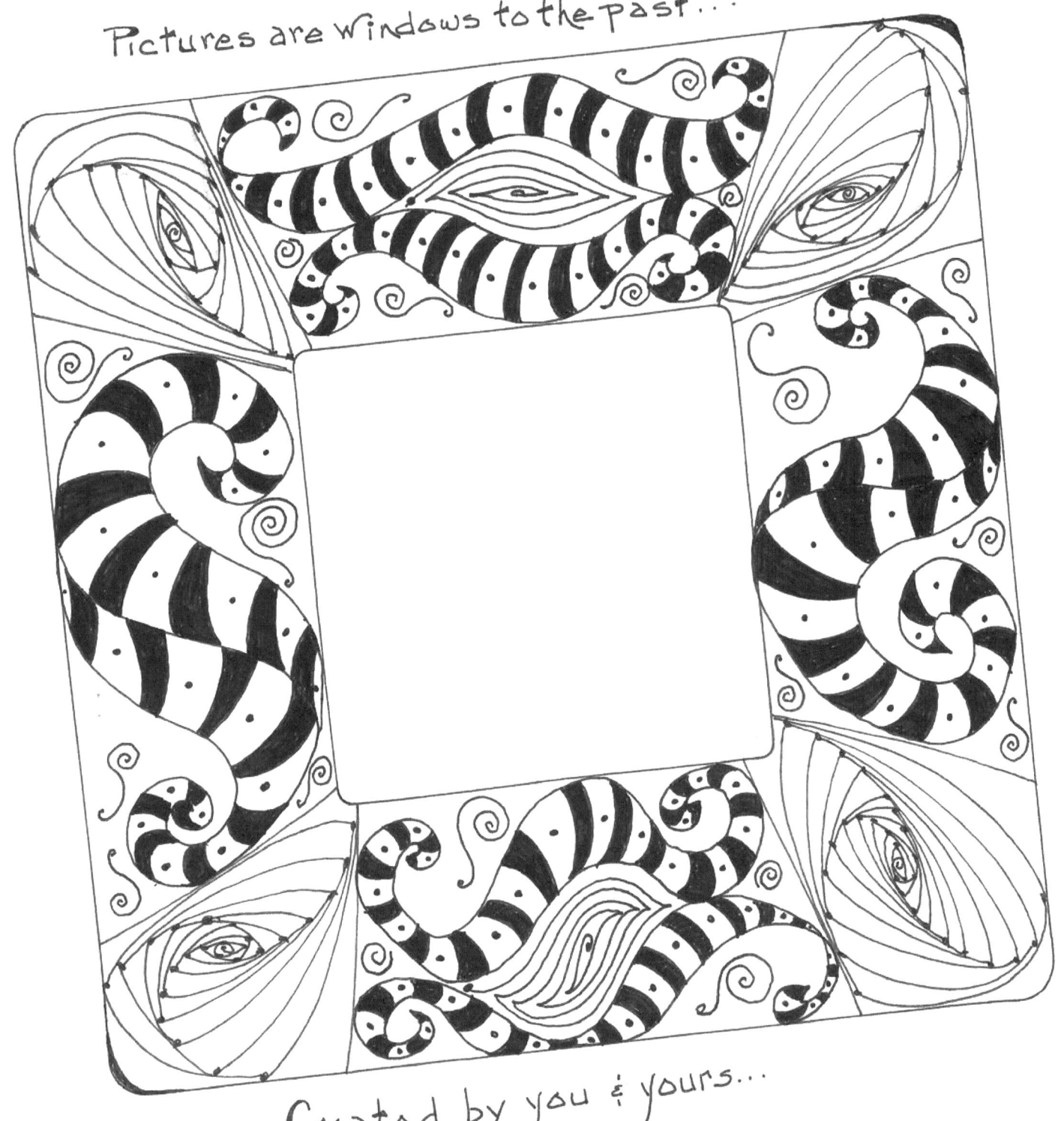

Created by you & yours...

Create yours here... :)

(14)

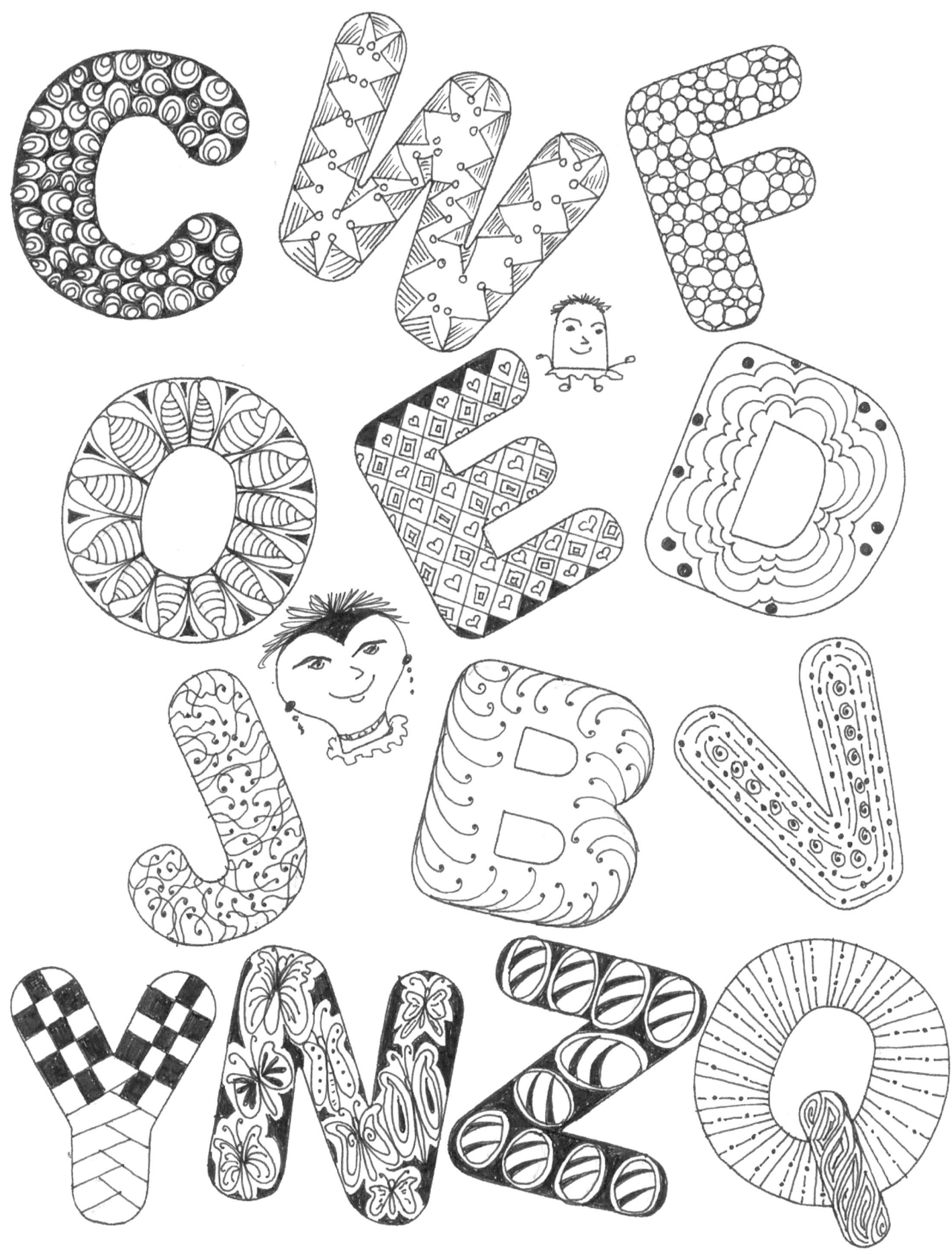

(15)

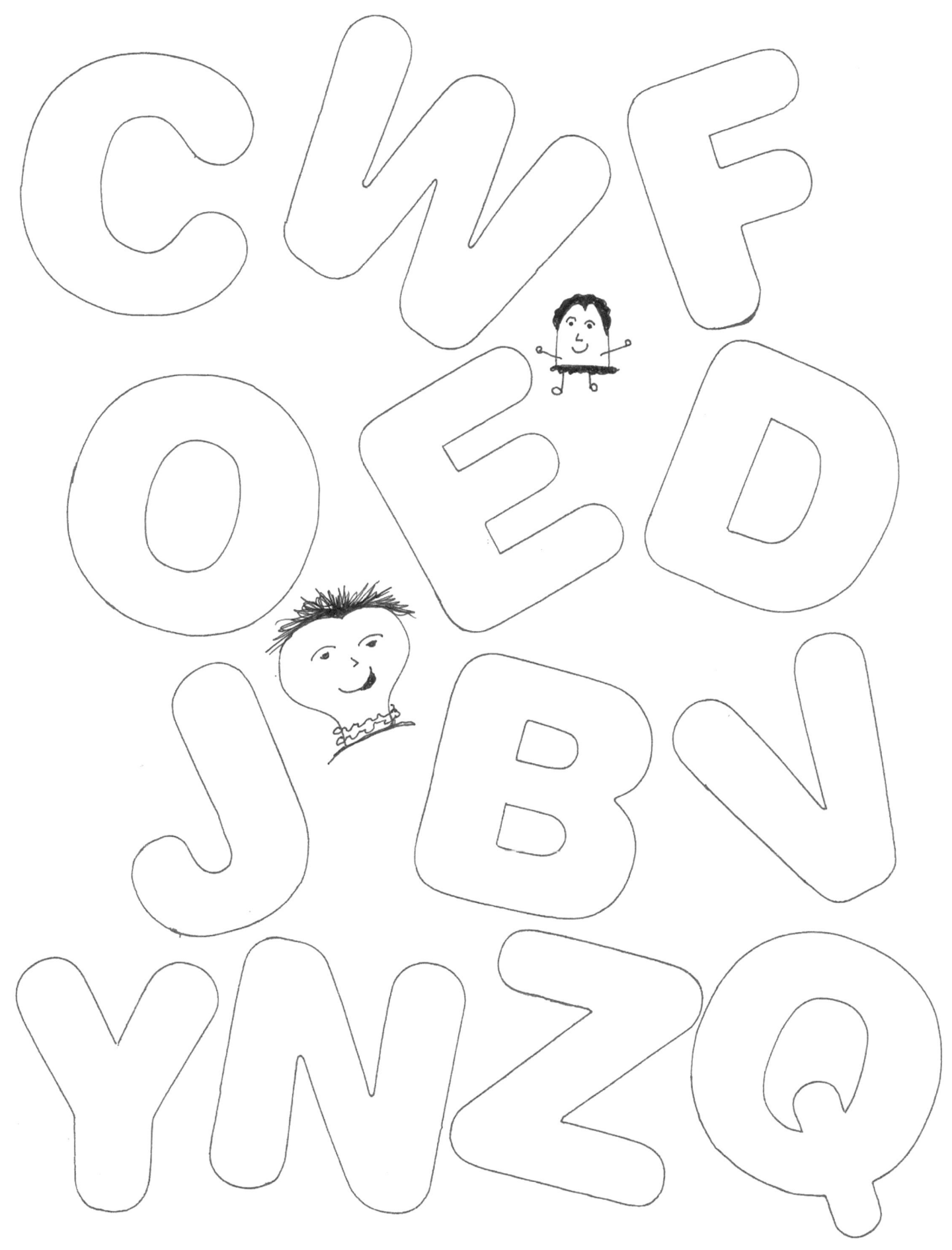

Letters...lots of letters. Color them, tangle them, copy them, have some fun!

Some ideas

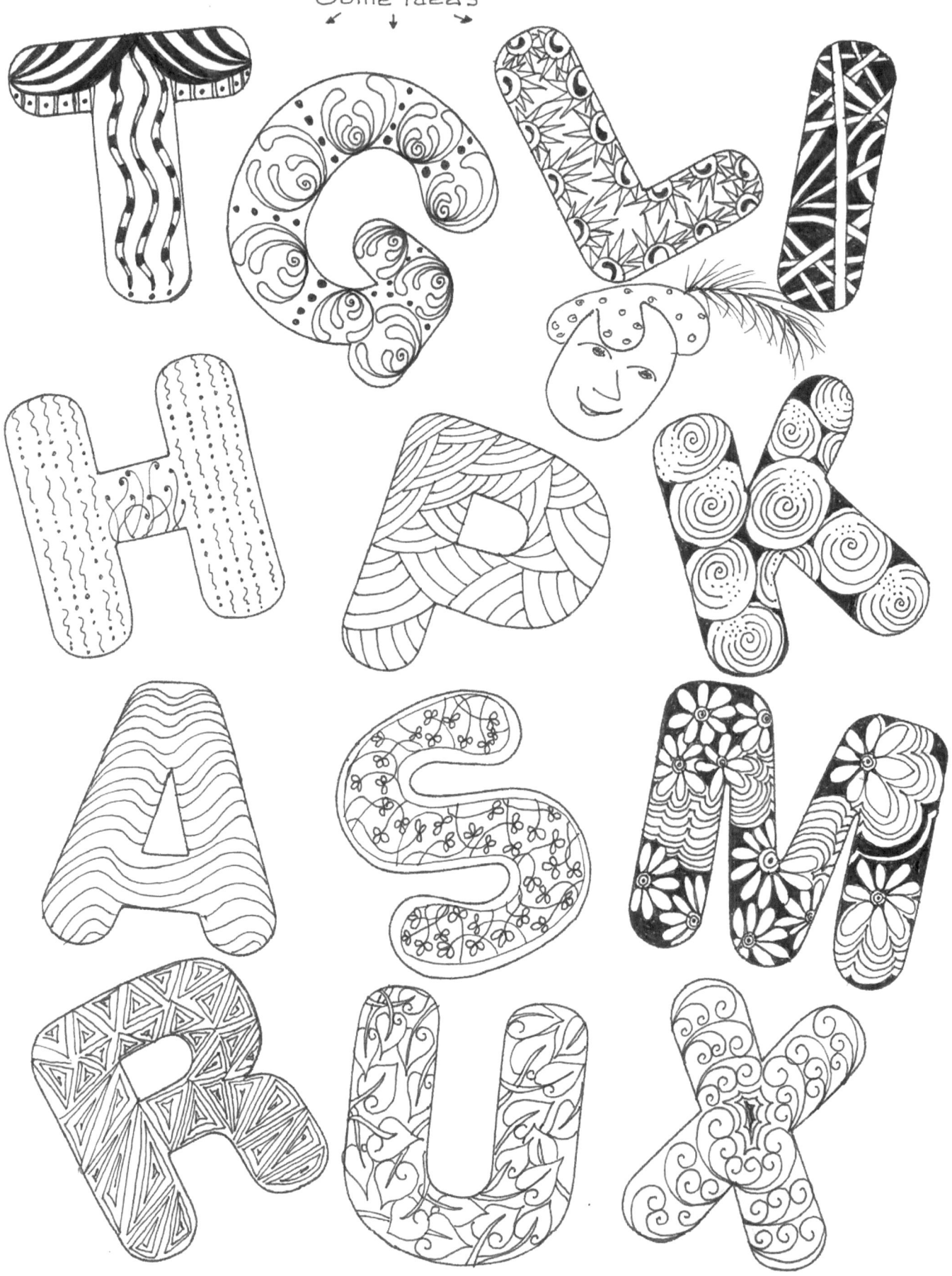

Letters...lots of letters. Color them, tangle them, copy them, have some fun!

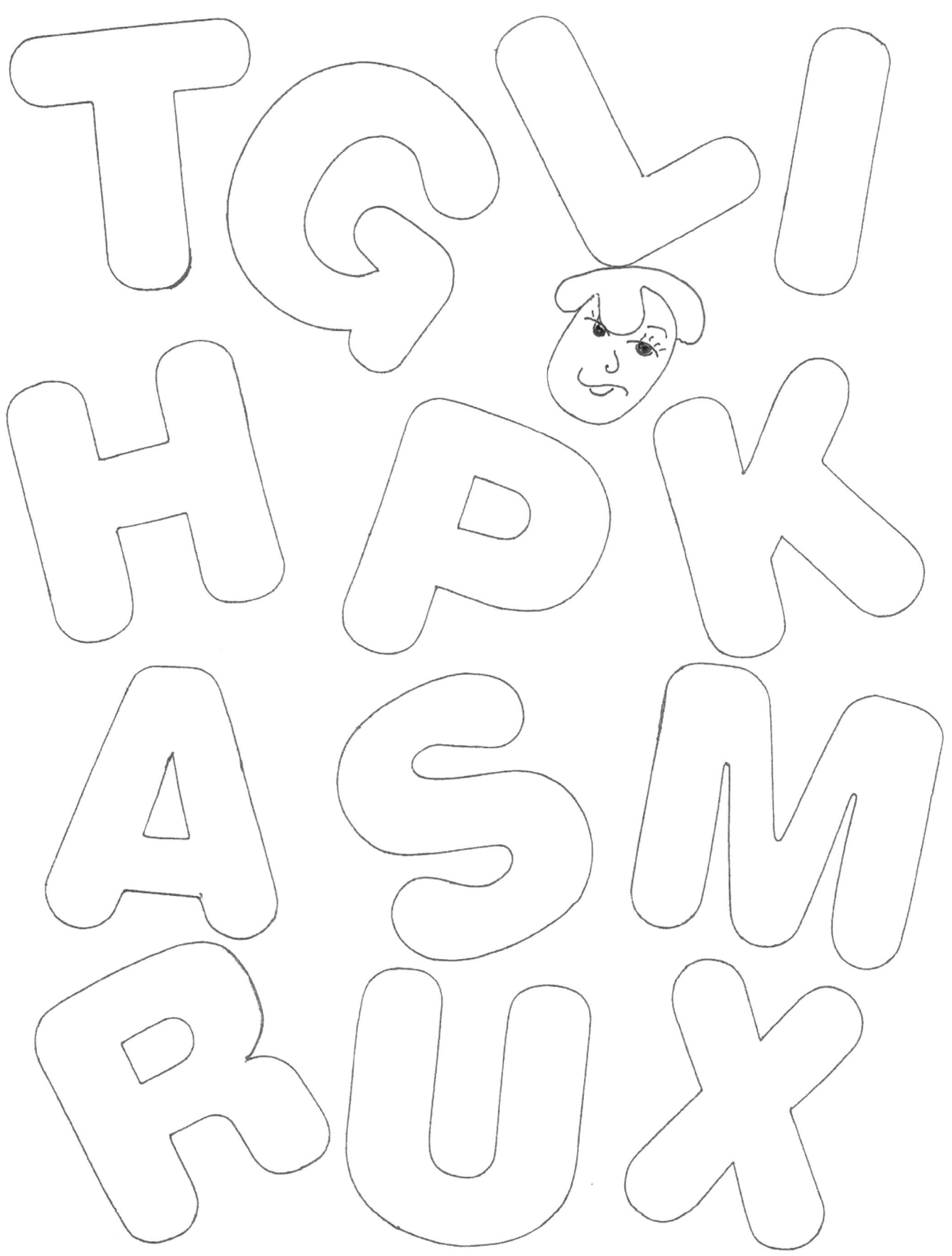

Circles within one another, halved, quartered and whole, create interest that leads the eye around the shapes.

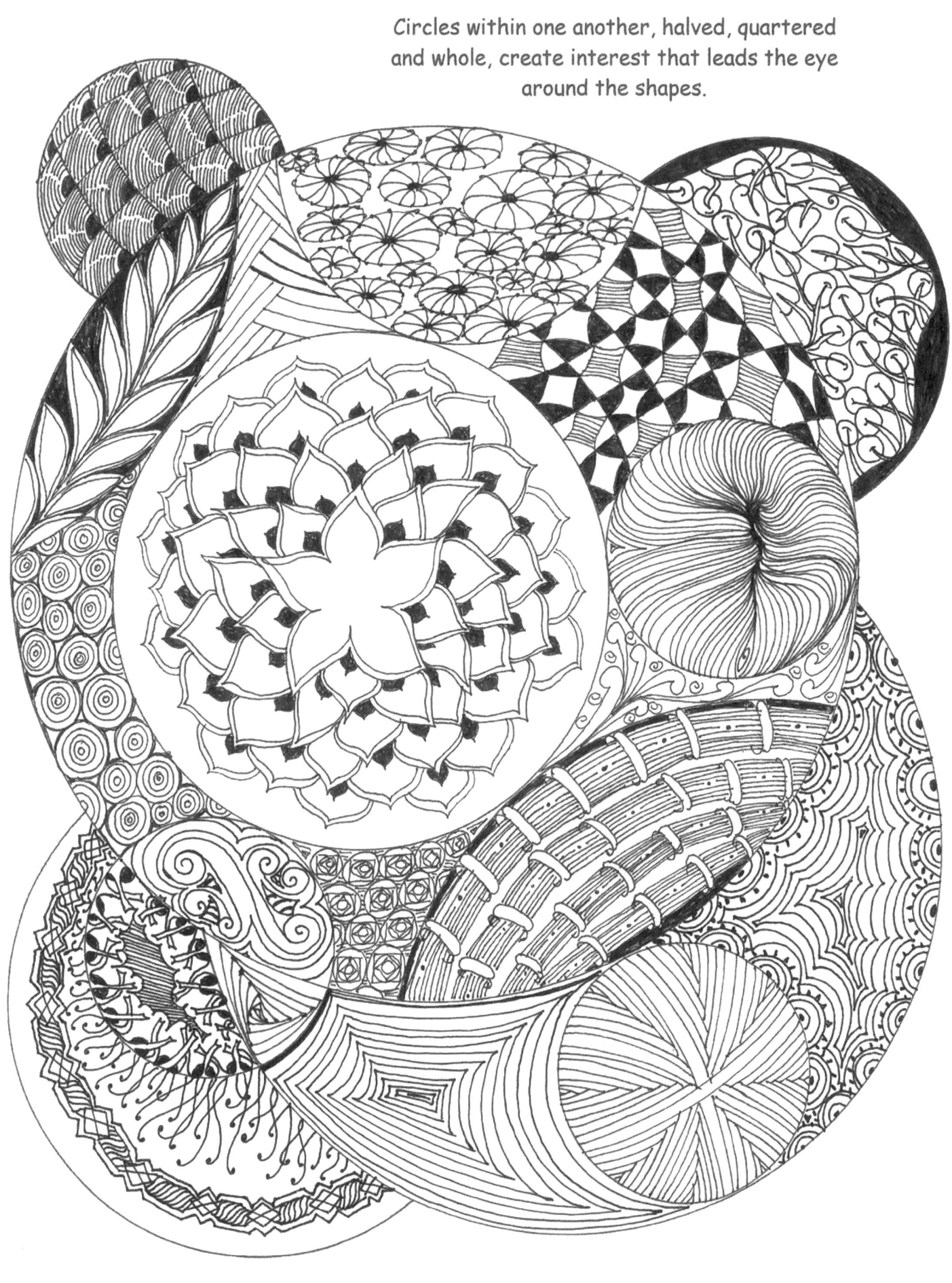

(19)

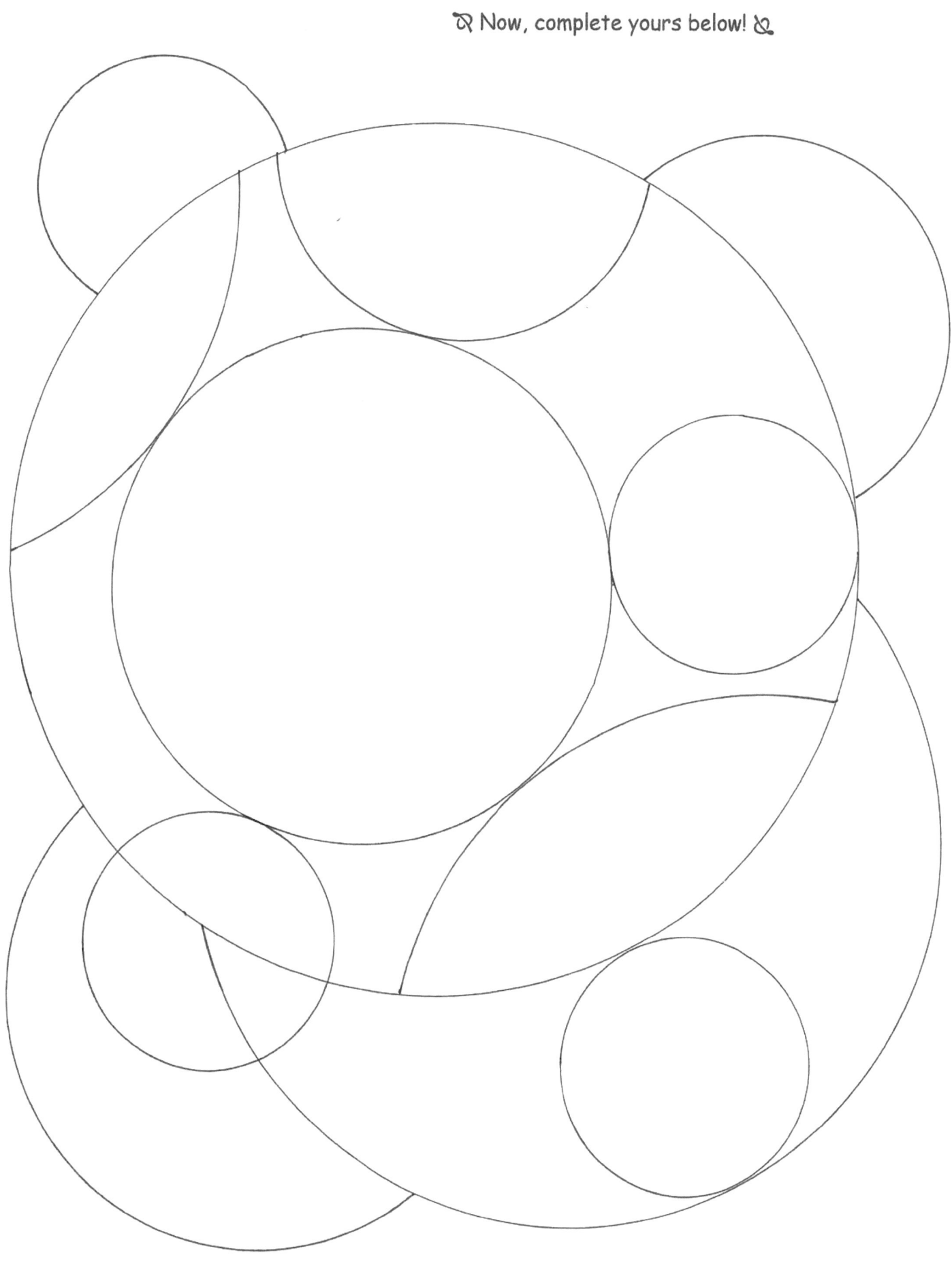

(20)

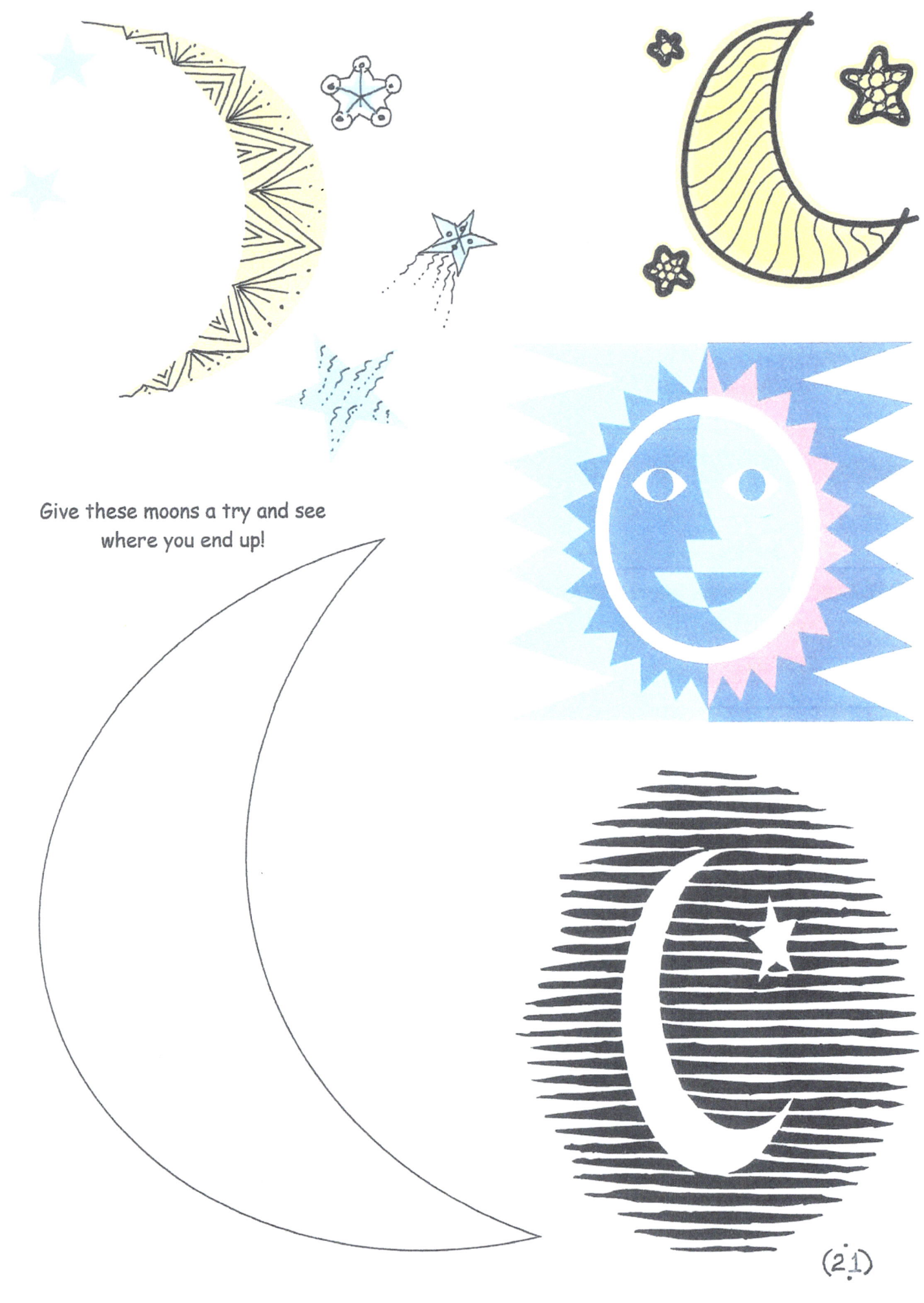

Give these moons a try and see where you end up!

The shapes below were made using a
Staedtler textures template. They
were fun to work with and due to the
templates durability, it can be used
again and again for lots of projects.

Fill in these

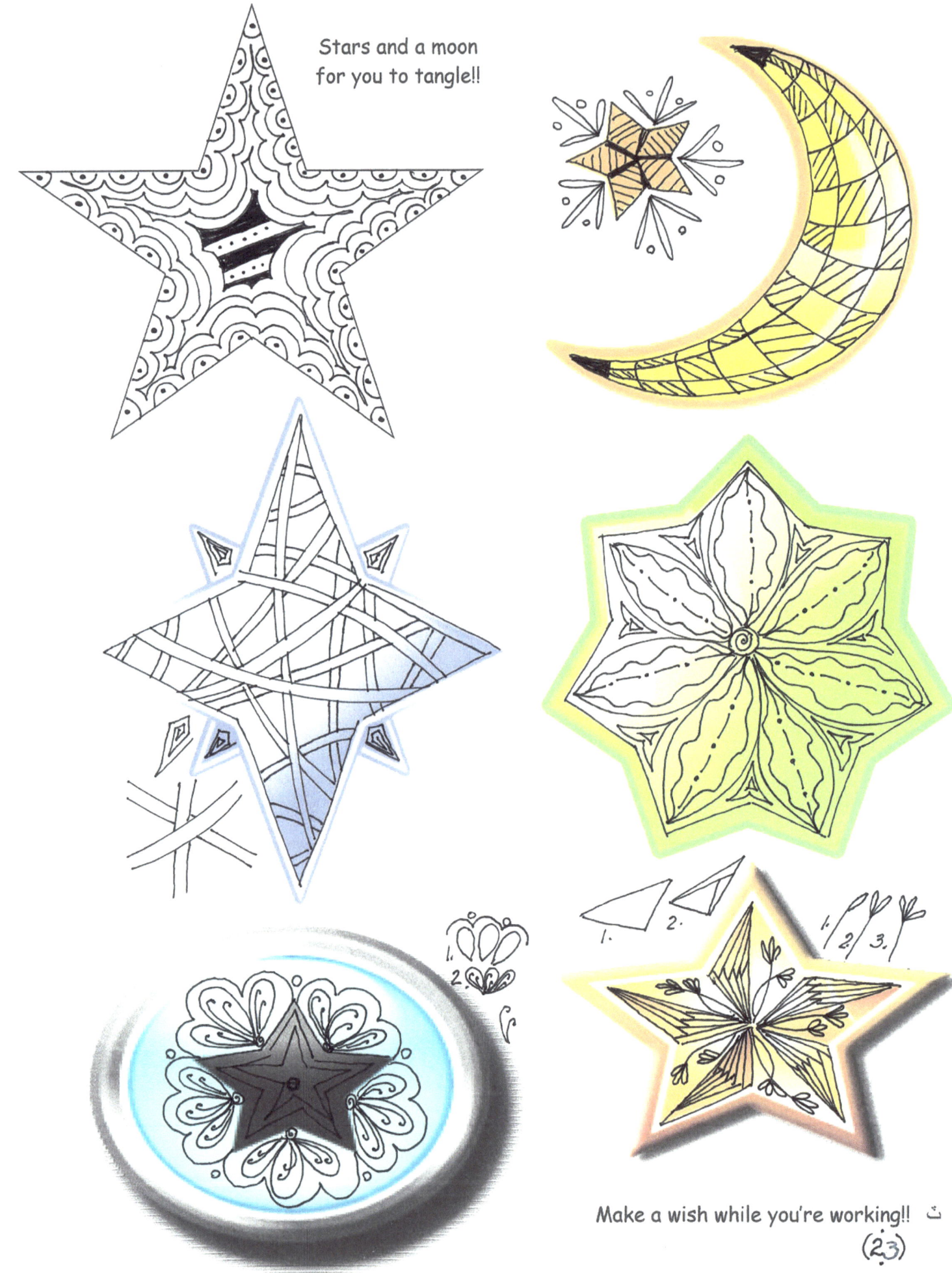

Stars and a moon for you to tangle!!

Make a wish while you're working!! ☺

(23)

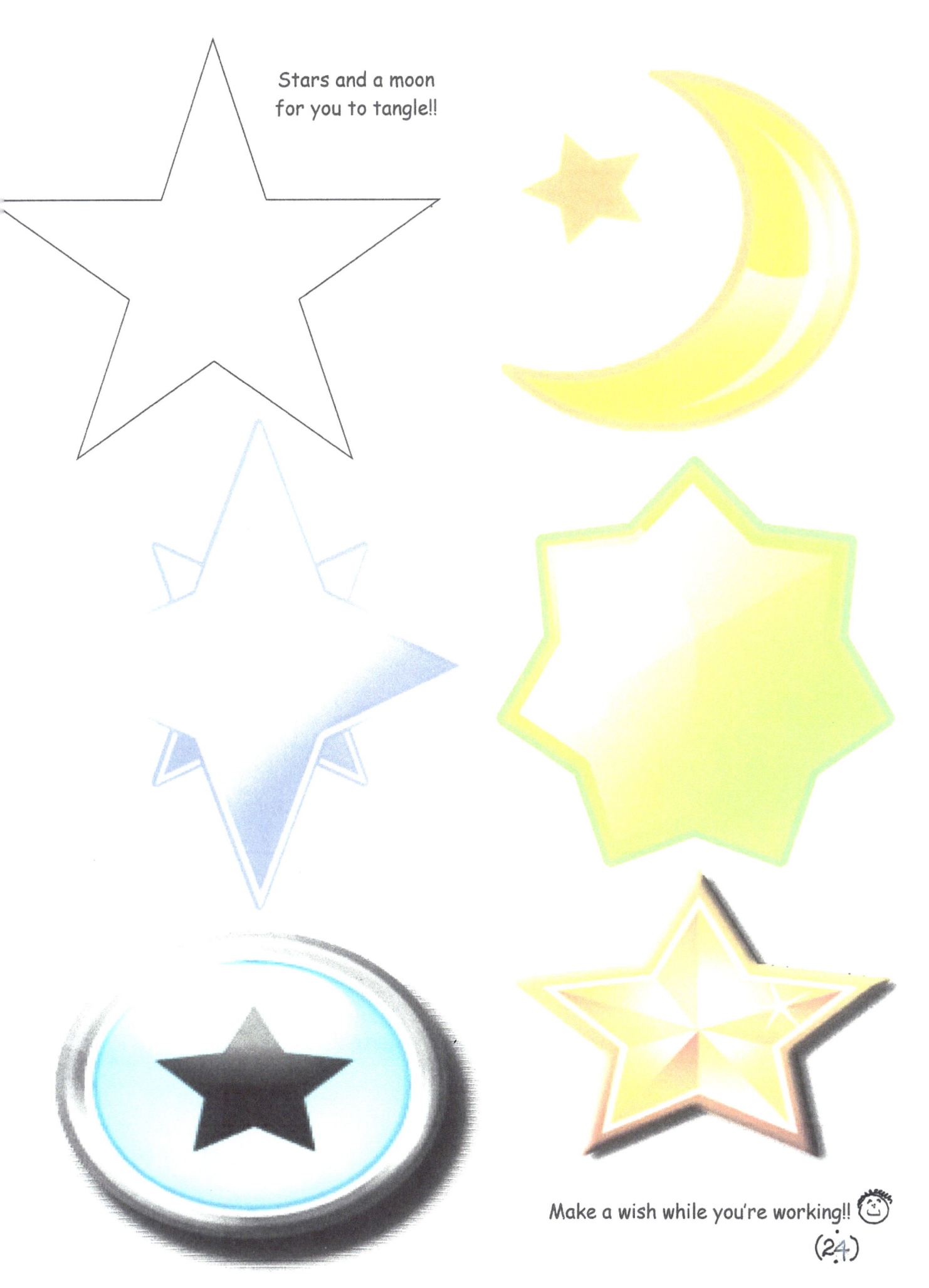

Stars and a moon for you to tangle!!

Make a wish while you're working!!

(24)

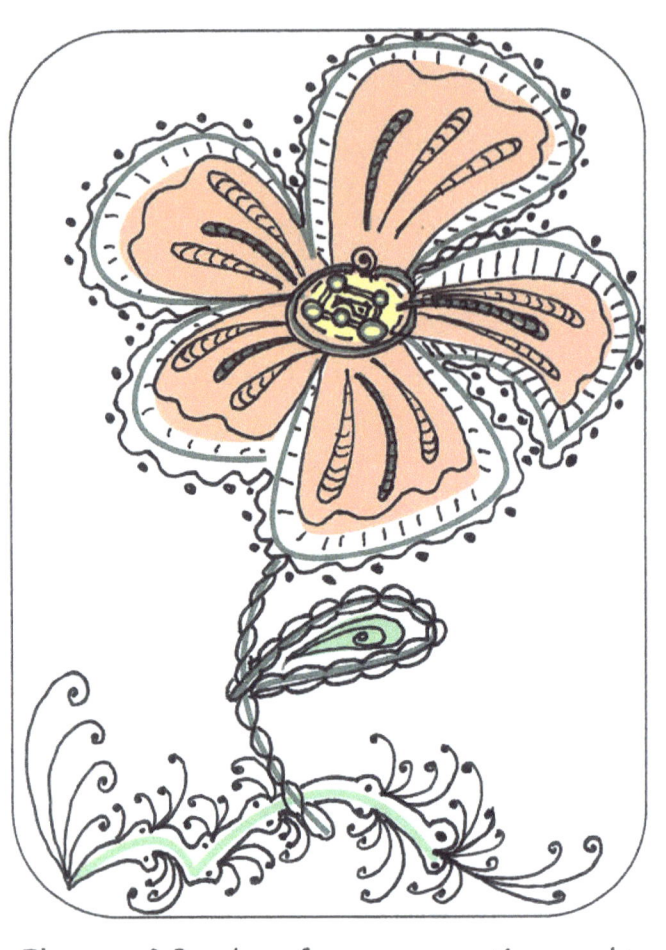

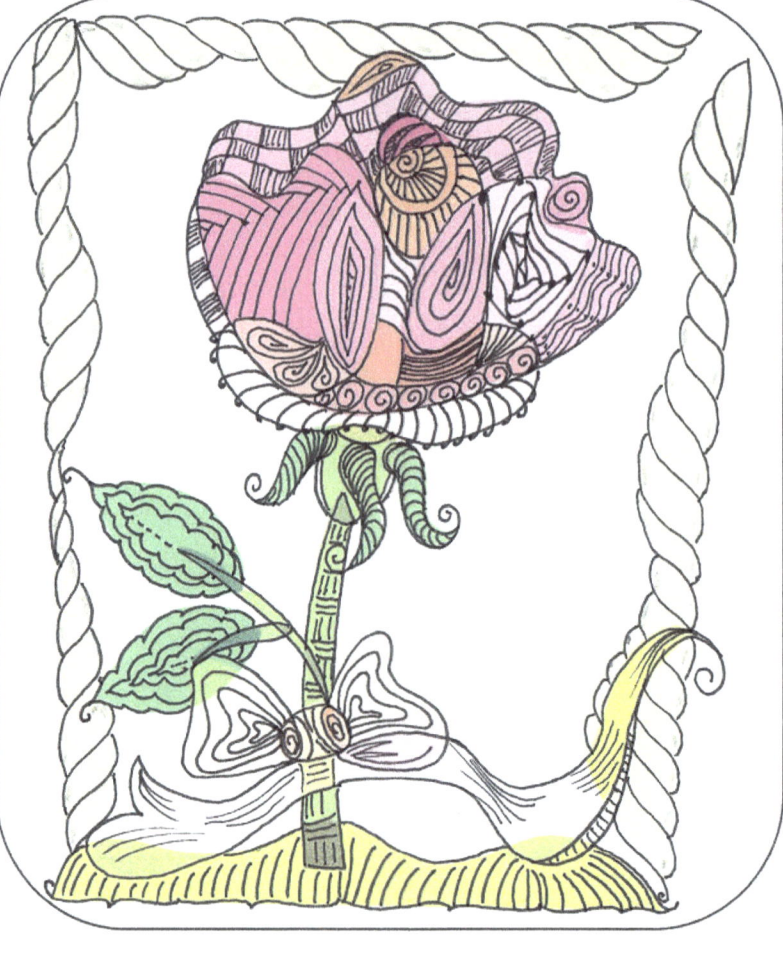

Flowers & Borders for your greeting cards.

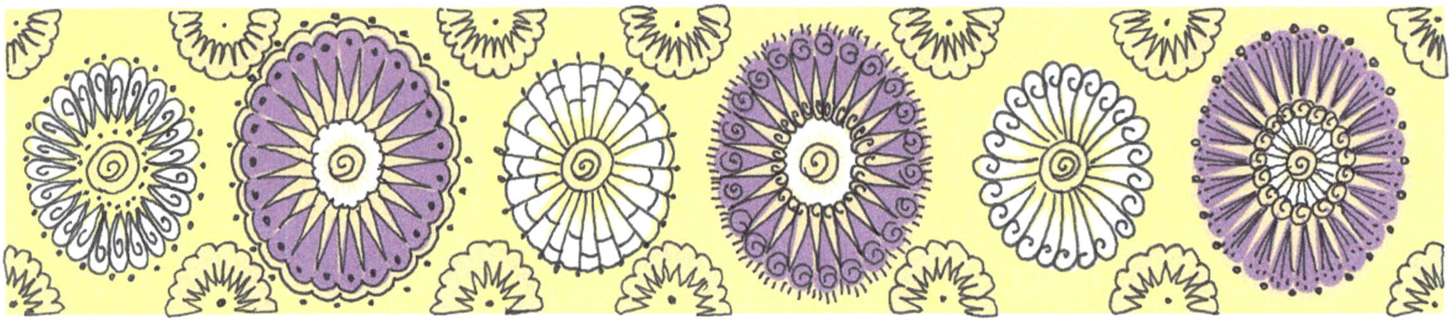

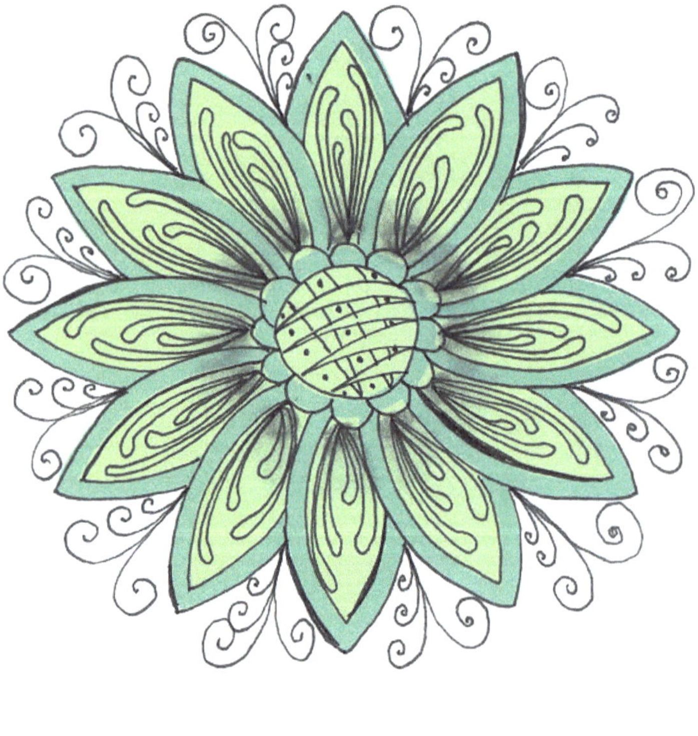

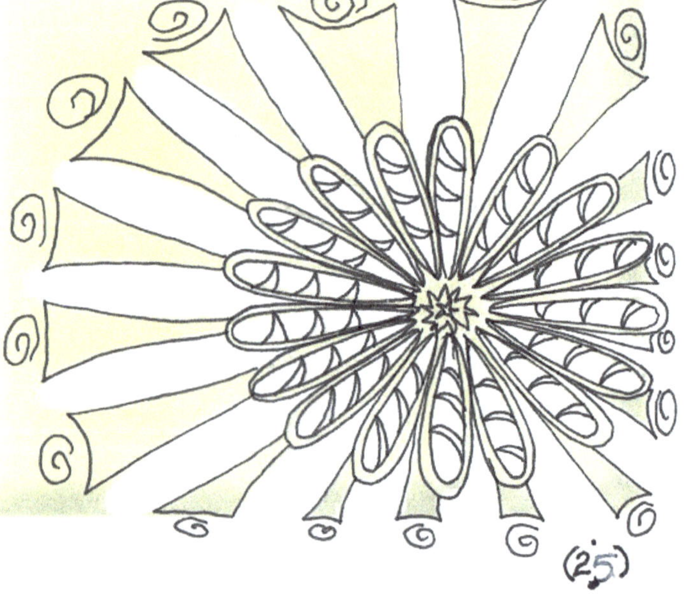

(25)

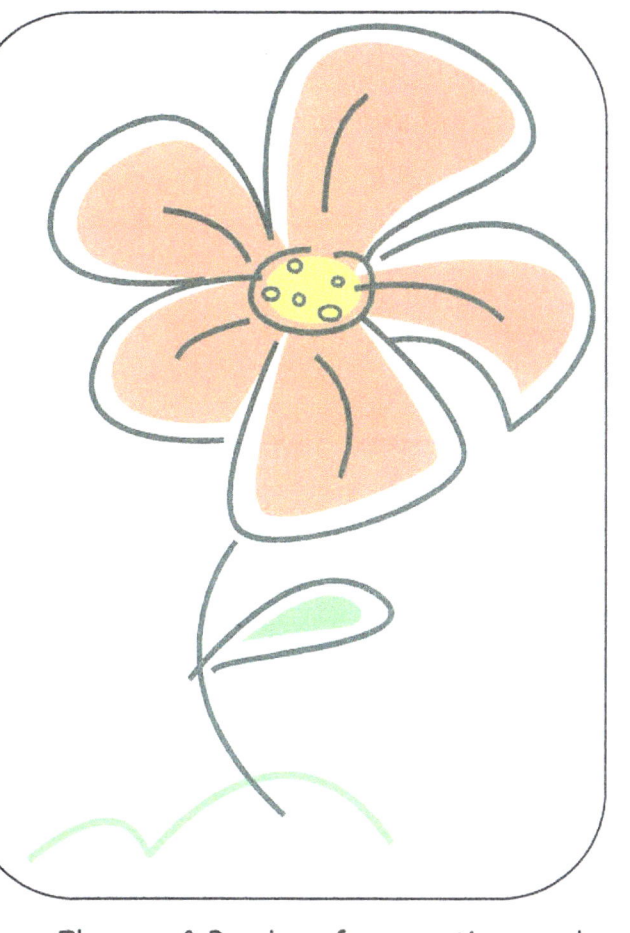

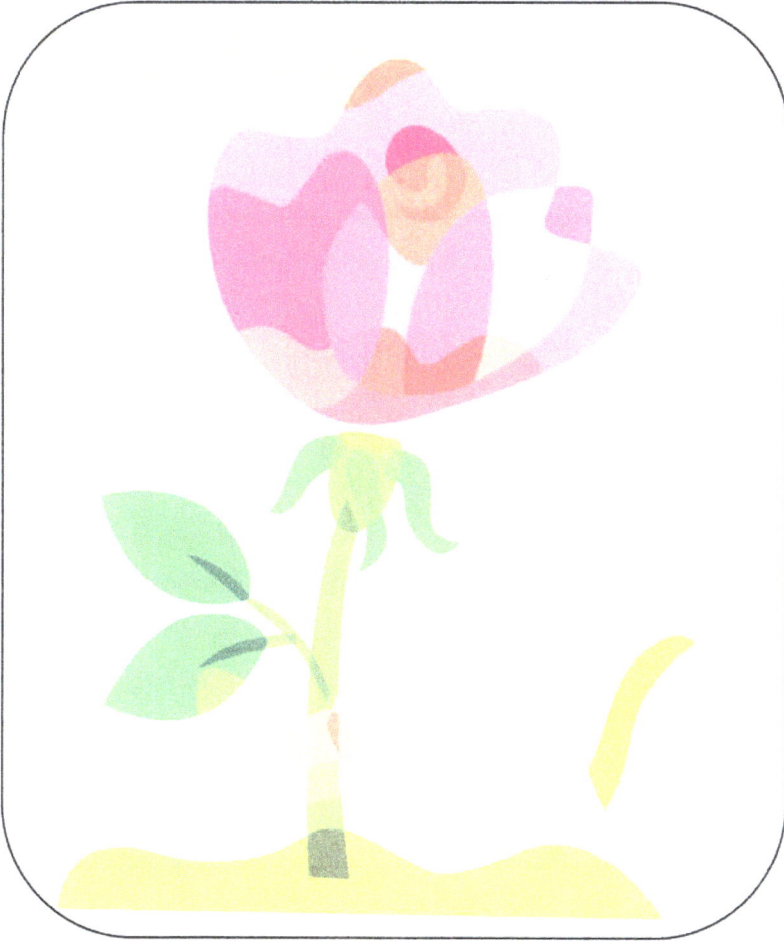

Flowers & Borders for greeting cards.

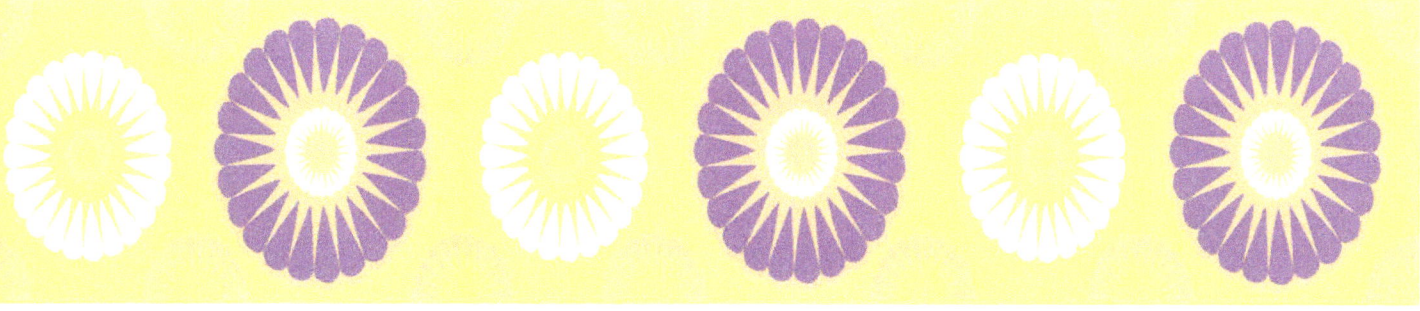

Tangle these!!!

(26)

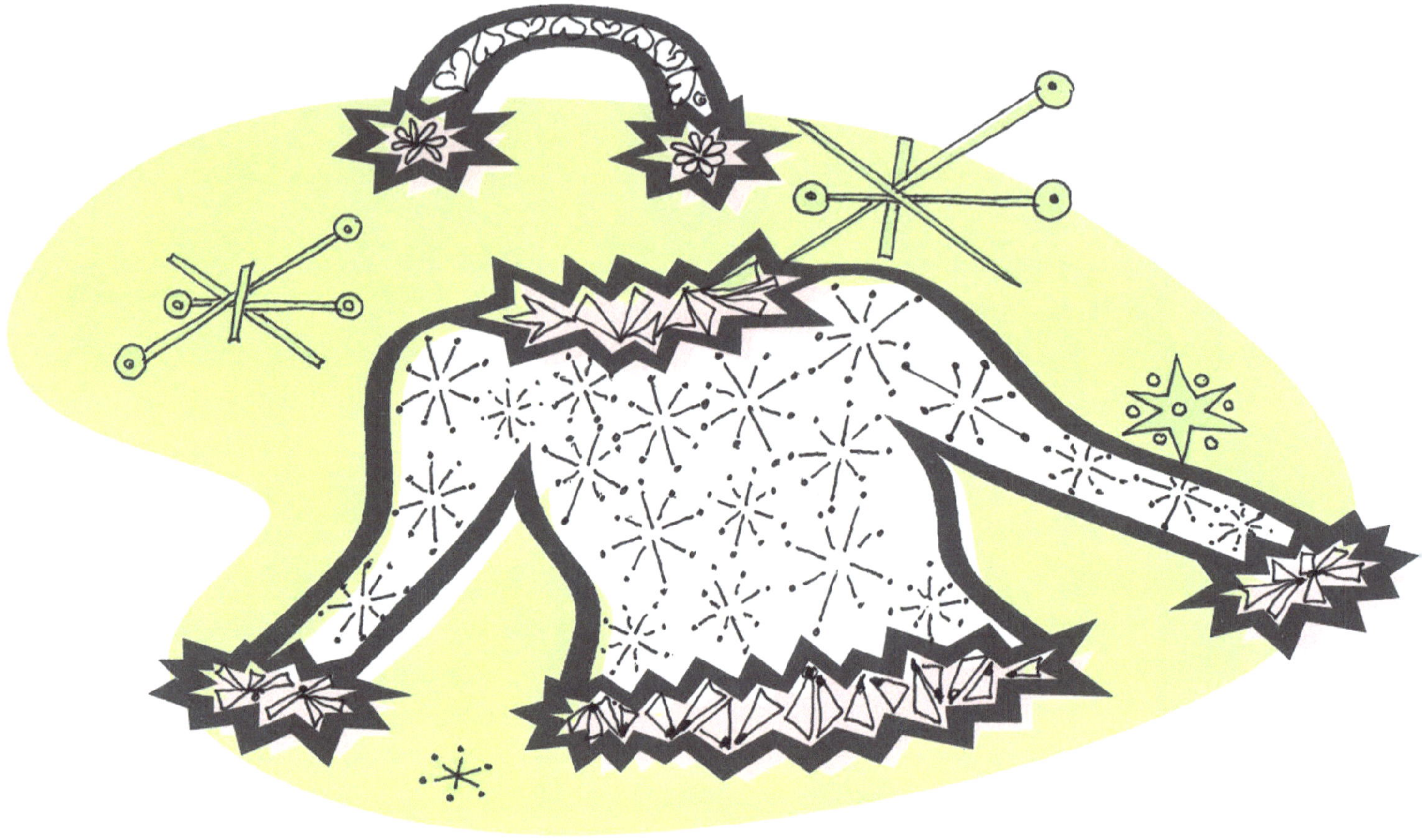

Here's a challenge for you...take an old pair of shoes or a piece of clothing and tangle it! It's great fun

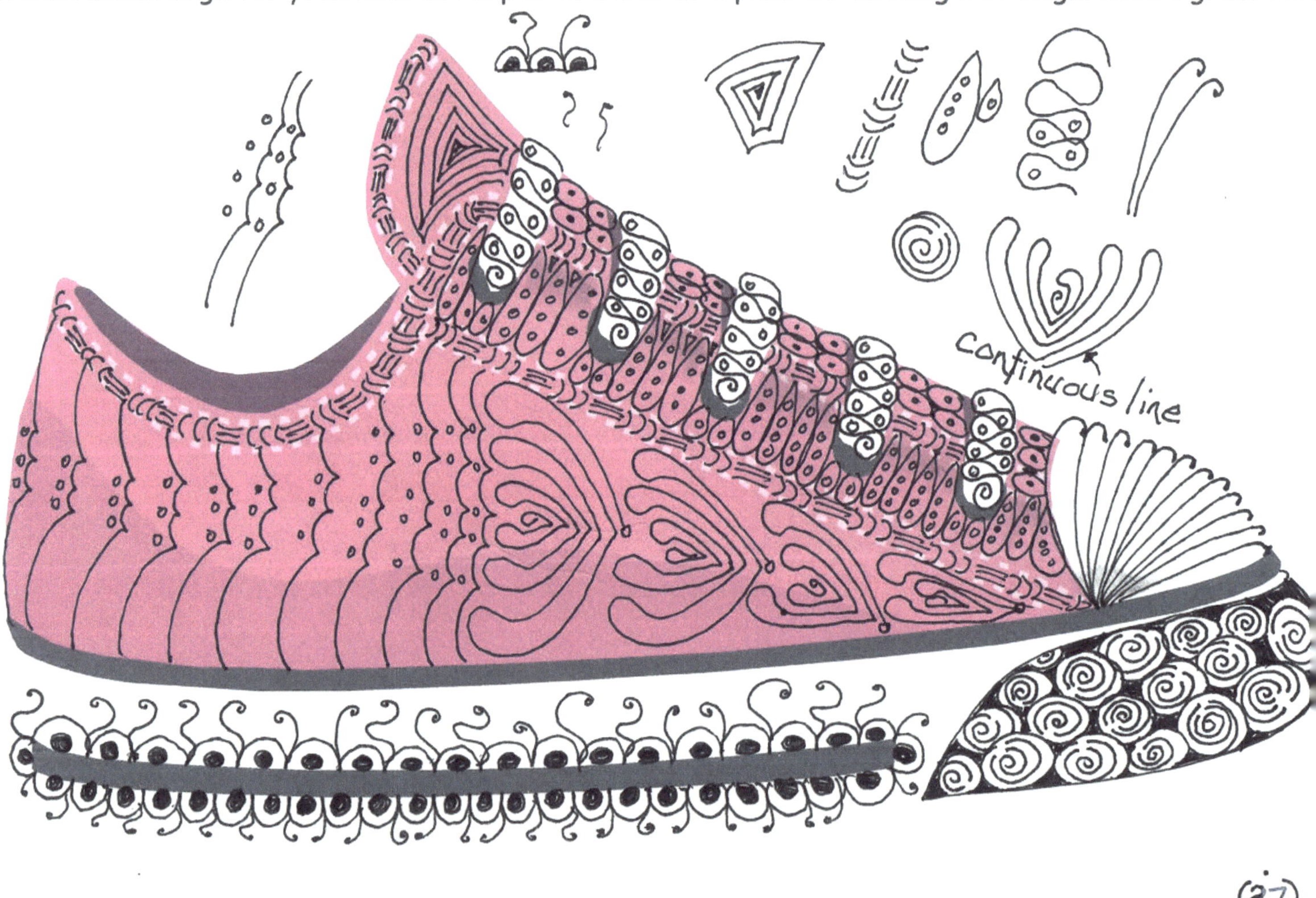

continuous line

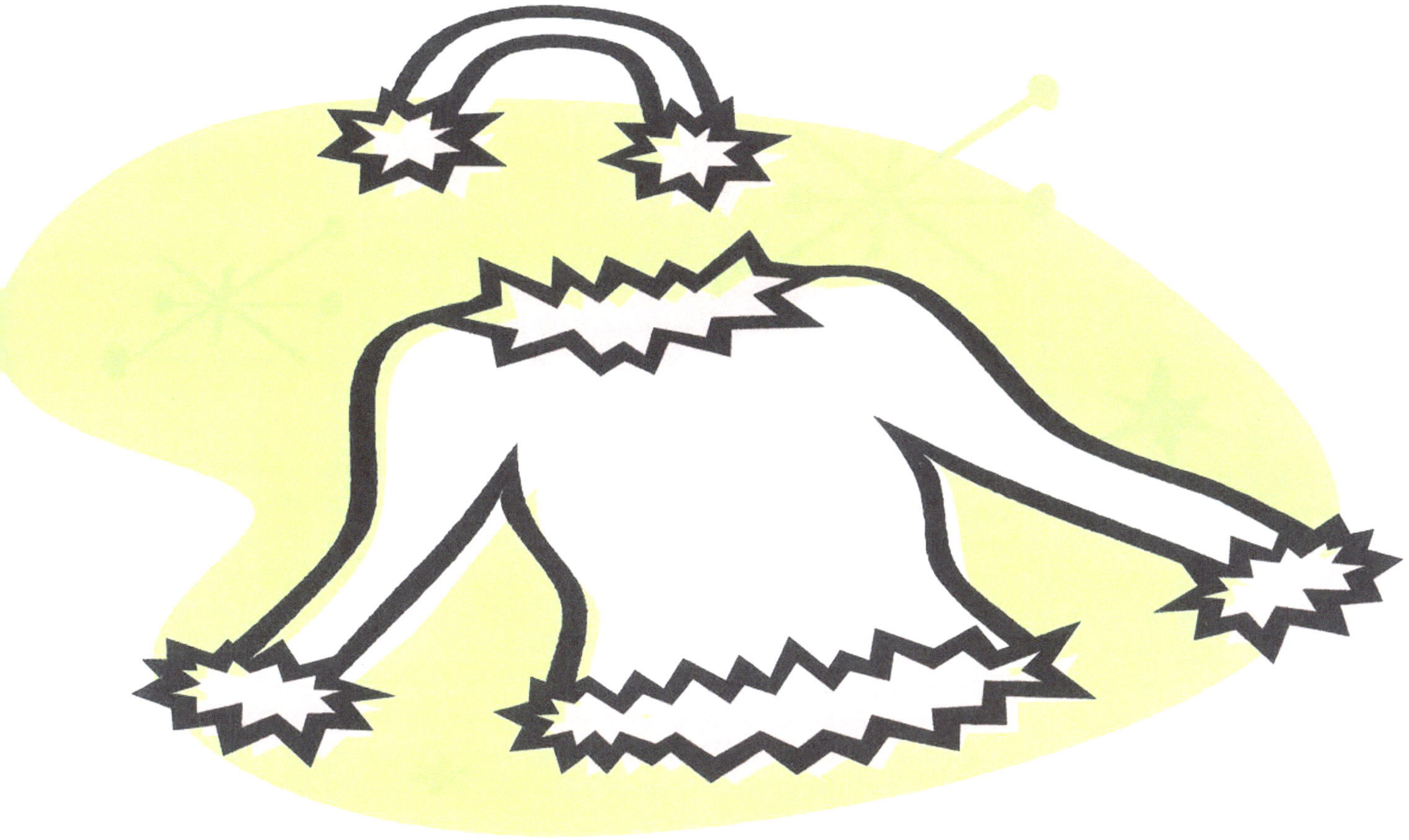

Practice on these...

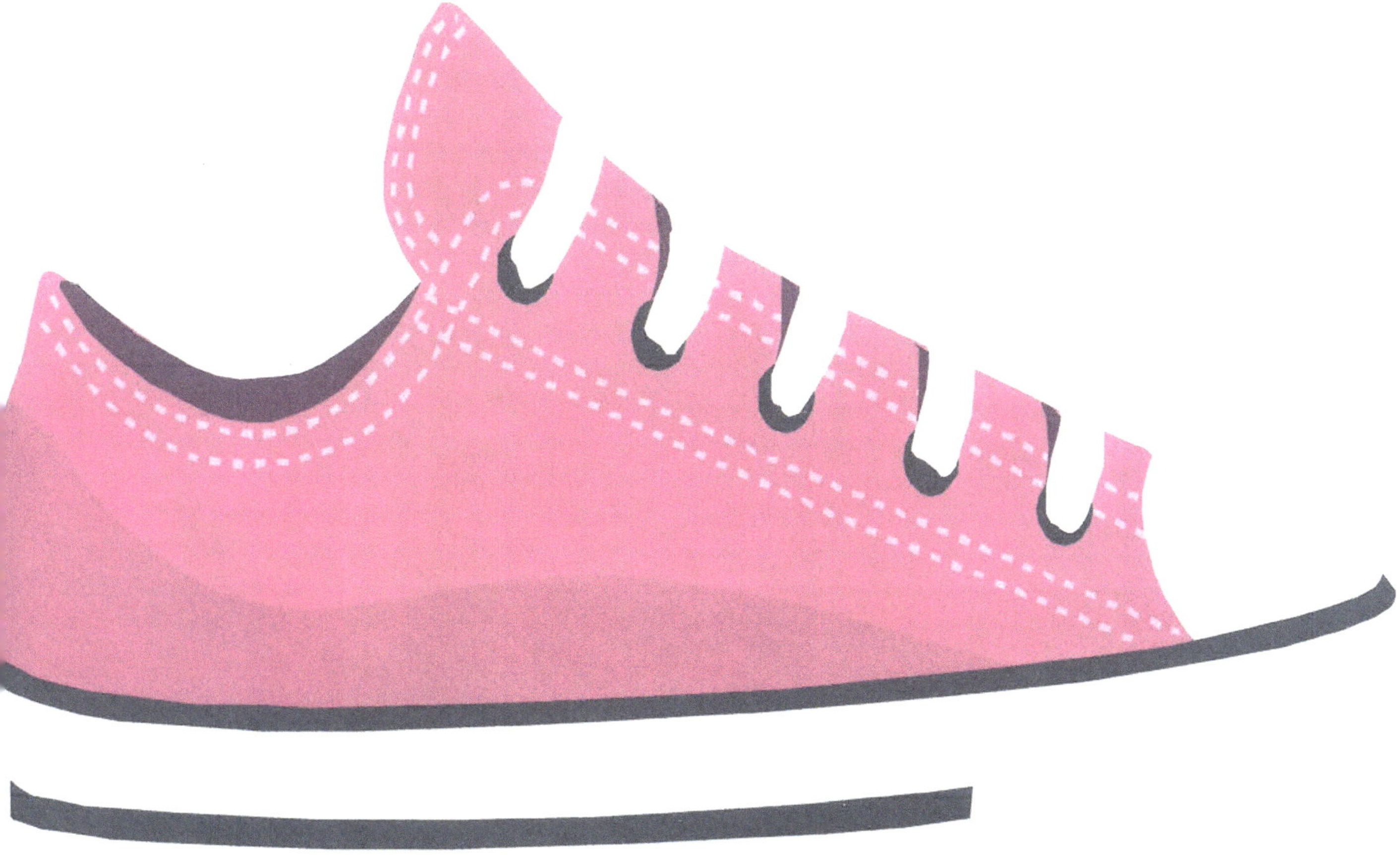

A tangled cat or two can be fun!
Add your own tangles on this cat page!

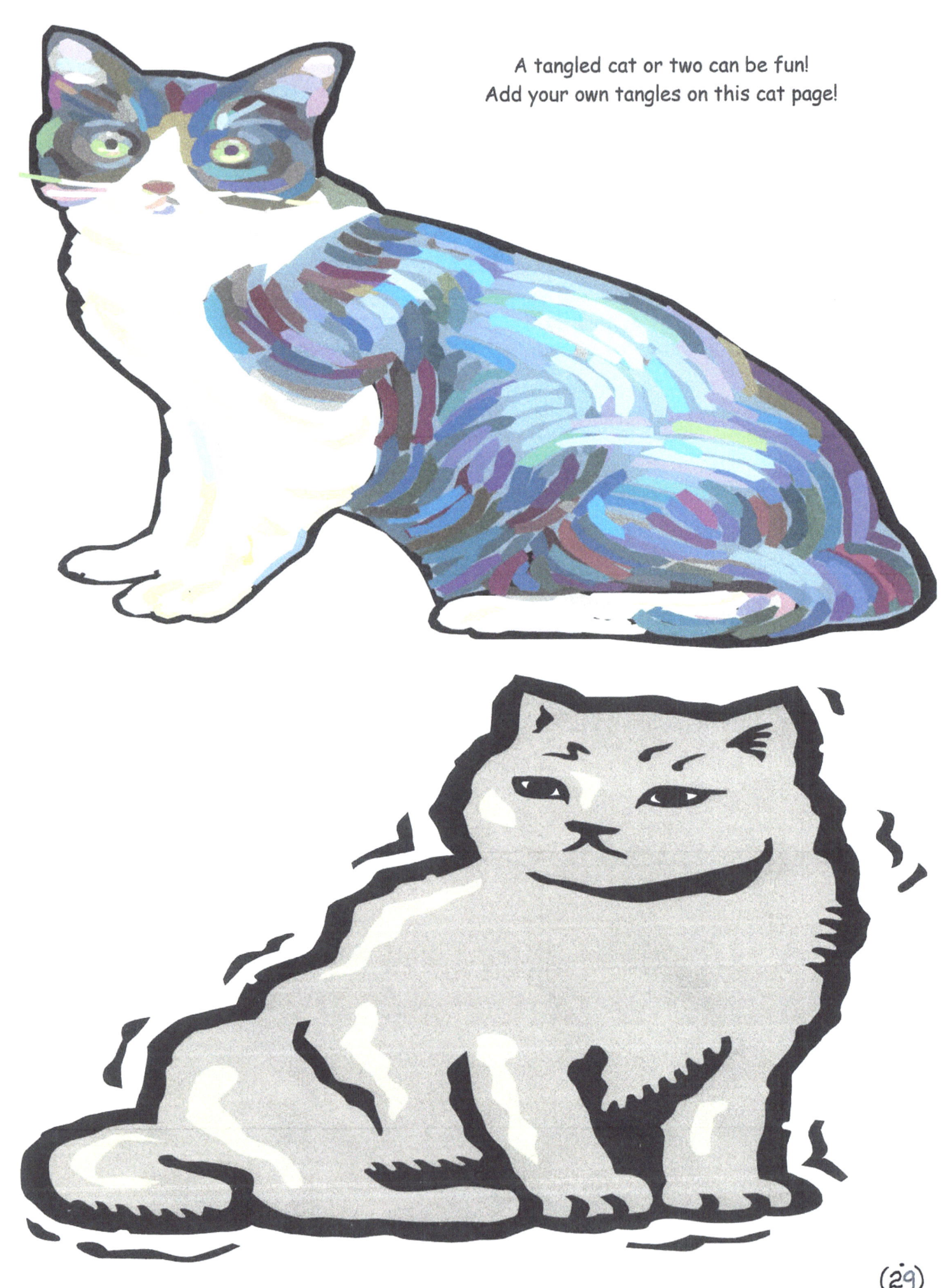

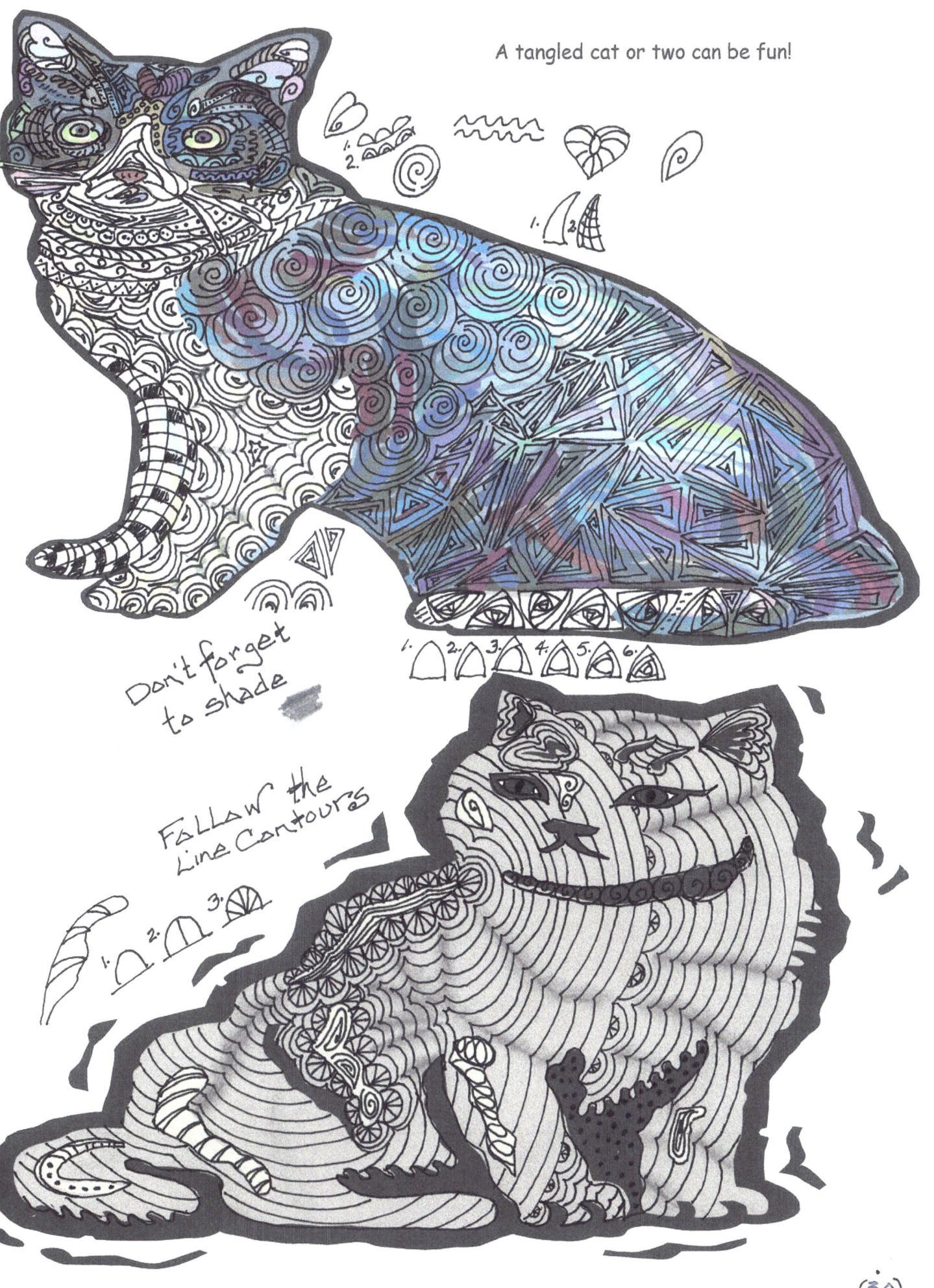

A tangled cat or two can be fun!

Don't forget to shade

Follow the line Contours

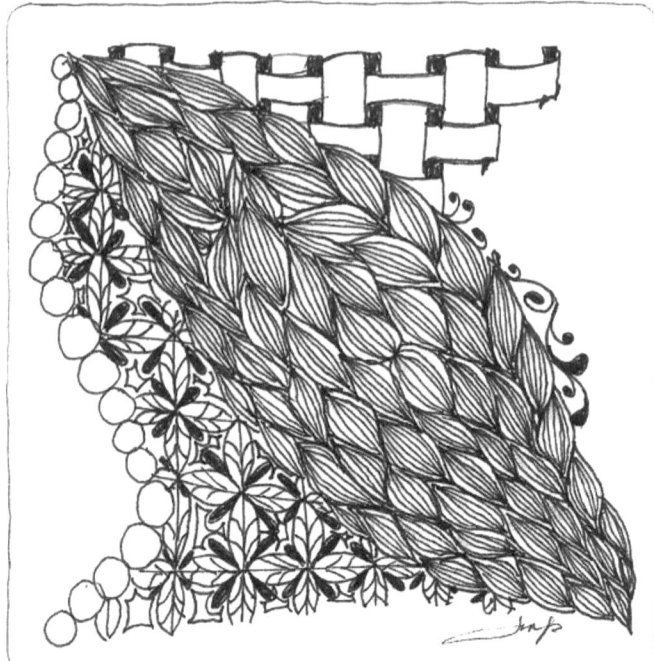

Extra's
for
you!

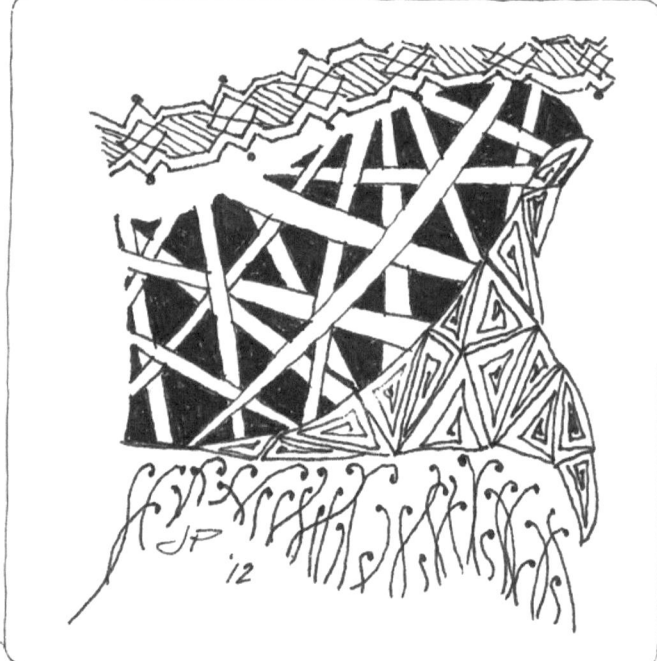

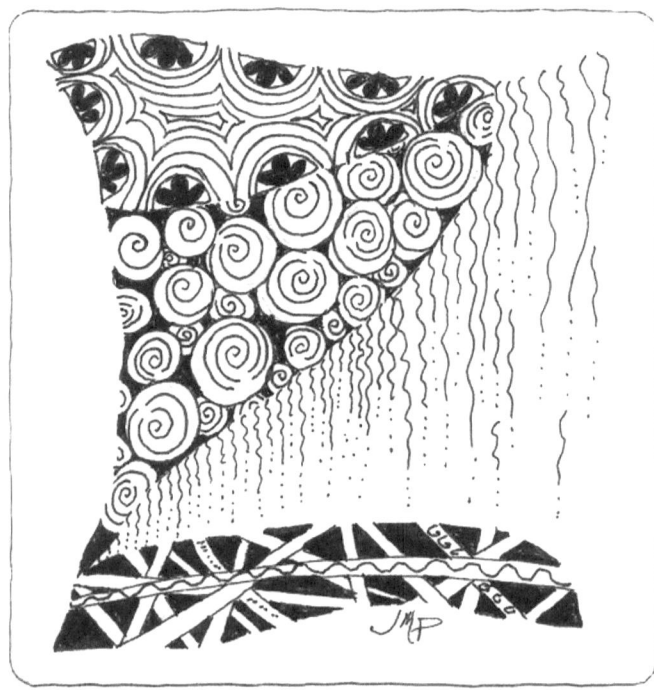